WEAPONS OF OUR WARFARE

SPIRITUAL STRATEGIES

BOOK I

JOHN LOPEZ

CONTENTS

First published in the United States of America by John Lopez

simplestrategies.jal@gmail.com

Library of Congress Cataloging-in-Publication data

A catalogue record for this book is available from the Library of Congress.

Designed and typeset by Lancelot Schaubert

Cover design by Lancelot Schaubert

Cover image by 卡晨 on Unsplash

ISBN — 979-8-9953105-0-1

e-book ISBN — 979-8-9953105-1-8

Printed in the United States of America.

CHAPTER 1

WHAT RESPONSE IS NEEDED

In the chaos of the modern world, there is often a question that is subtly asked: "What response is needed?" There are so many options and distractions in every situation. With networking, social life, conflict, and prayer, it is important to understand that time is a valuable commodity. It is not possible to produce biblical fruit without being mindful of our responses to every situation. The spiritual realm, much like the physical realm, is active and requires just as much awareness and a thoughtful response. If the church is going to remain healthy, congregation leaders must be vigilant and look for every opportunity to be obedient to God; therefore, when it comes to spiritual warfare as well, Christians need to ask, "What response is needed?"

Christians have the job and goal to be obedient to God. We need to be active in practicing vigilance, listening, praying, and searching for new ways to bring about His kingdom on earth. I have been praying and seeking God while studying Scripture. In my quiet time, I have found what I believe to be effective strategies key for fighting against the powers of the enemy at this time. These Bible passages point to a very different type of response, when dealing with specific "spirits," than I have heard taught in congregations. Before we define what a spirit is though, we need to establish a baseline strategy for responding.

I have discovered, during my time in church, that many people try to deal with certain sins or temptations by choosing a behavior that seems to be the opposite of a particular sin or temptation. For instance, they might fight pride with humility, lust with purity, or greed with generosity. While these strategies may be of some value, I do not believe, from my studies, that what we perceive to be the opposite behavior is always accurate. Addressing the source of temptation is also necessary. If you have a cough, it does not mean that you have a cold: There can be many reasons for a cough, and each one may require a different treatment. Likewise, while some responses may help to address personal sins and temptations, should the response change when the source of temptation is not of the flesh but from the enemy? If we misdiagnose the spirit or misunderstand the nature of a spirit, then we may be fighting a losing battle. What is the best response if an external spirit is trying to tempt a man or a woman to lust, rather than if they are personally struggling with sexual desire?

Sometimes an "opposite" spirit may be the solution; but the problem frequently is that what we believe to be the opposite of an issue may be a misunderstanding of the problem. For instance, we might think that the opposite of slavery is freedom; but if we change the frame of reference from the slave to the master, the opposite of slavery becomes empowerment. If we think of concepts in terms of opposites, then we might also fail to grasp their depth or nuance. If we define light as the lack of darkness, and darkness as the lack of light, we fail to understand the nature of light separately from the definition of darkness. Light is a wave and a particle: it exists as a spectrum of color and degrees of energy. If the only definition of a virtue is based on its vice, then they are equal in value. For this reason, it is helpful to think about vices and virtues not as opposites but more as seeds that, when planted, grow into behaviors that help to defend against or weaken different areas of temptation. Finally, it's important to understand the difference between a source and fruit. We need to establish that we are responding to the source and stopping the symptoms or behavior, rather than just trying to produce one that appears to be the opposite.

This book will address dealing with spirits in a biblical way. God, as a healer, knows how to heal people and will often address the heart of a matter while ignoring the symptoms. Christians must learn to identify the root of a problem to target it appropriately. If we fight against the symptoms of temptation but allow the spirit of lust into our midst, we are going to be fighting a losing battle. So, an appropriate question would be "How does someone know if they are fighting a spirit or their own flesh?" The best answer would be simply to ask God and seek Him first. There are some clues that can inform leaders and intercessors who can expose the enemy. The questions that children of God ask are the most important part of this process because unless they ask appropriate questions, they will rarely get the answers they are looking for.

To understand which questions are the right ones, we must understand what the questions imply. A question is not just a sentence that elicits a response. It is also a diagnostic tool that can be used to understand how the person who asks thinks. For instance, by asking the question "What must I do to be good?" the asker has already displayed many assumptions. One assumption is that they assume that they are capable of goodness; another is that goodness is a product of an action. Both ideas could very well be lies. If this is the case, then the question itself must be discarded. Questions must expose the ignorance of the asker if they desire a meaningful answer.

When asking God questions, Christians 'with confidence draw near to the throne of grace' (Hebrews 4:16) and ask questions that assume they know nothing: nothing except what God has taught them. If a man or woman asks God a question based on something that they assume to be true, then the response will often not lead to understanding. An example of this is when the Pharisees asked Jesus if it was required to pay taxes to Rome (Matthew 22:15–22). The question assumed that to pay the taxes was to submit to bondage, but to reject the tax was to act unlawfully. In this way, the question was asked to elicit a yes or no answer and did not leave any room for the truth of the matter to be exposed. So, when Jesus answered, He uncovered the wicked desire in the Pharisees' hearts, while also revealing their ignorance. They had a carnal view about submission to God; Jesus was showing that they must serve God with their whole being, as opposed to Caesar, who was to be served only to the extent of the law on earth.

Often, when God speaks, He doesn't answer how we expect Him to. When He responds, He usually does so to the intention behind the question. Even when an individual asks God, "Do you love me?" it is not uncommon for them to be met by waves of approval or perhaps a vision of God revealing His desire for that person. God wants people to understand the love He has for them, not to casually accept it as a reality. So, when asking God questions, I suggest asking questions about who He is, how He feels, and what His desires are. When posing these questions, His responses will be a free expression of love and compassion for us and not limited by any constraints. We give God the opportunity to completely change our world views each time we speak to Him.

When a concern arises, it is important to understand our role, if any, in the response to a spiritual conflict. I would suggest starting by asking these three questions:

1. Is this something God is 'currently' trying to address?
2. Is this something affecting my community or only me? To what extent? Is it affecting my place/residence? Is it church-wide? Is it city-wide? Is it nationwide? Does it reflect the state of the world?
3. Is there a lingering sense of fear when I try to think about or strategize against this problem?

The first question is important because unless God is currently working on the problem, there is no grace for us to take it on. If we keep trying to fight the battles God is not asking us to fight, then there is no path to success. If God is our victory in all things, then we keep our eyes on where He is, and we will find the strength to fight.

If we do not have the peace to engage in spiritual warfare, then I would encourage us to do two things. First, seek God about which battles are ours; and second, ask God to empower us to endure. God is moving and has a purpose; it is important we align ourselves with that purpose if we are to find victory. For those of us who are driven and passionate about a specific concern or desire for breakthrough, seeking God and asking Him to stand with us helps us to keep our eyes on Him. God may reveal to us that He is very much fighting the battle we are looking at, but His approach may be considerably different. Therefore, seeking Him is the most important part of spiritual warfare. Asking the right questions is crucial to victory. If our battles lead us to spend more time looking at the enemy, then we are fighting in the wrong way.

The second question asks whether a problem is ours alone or whether it affects many people. If there is a problem with the community, then it is always spiritual. If a group of people are generous and caring, they are moving in a spirit of generosity. Likewise, if a congregation operates in gossip and slander, then they are collectively agreeing with a spirit of contention. With a community problem, the community should always respond together. This does not mean a personal or individual problem cannot be rooted in spiritual attack; but if there is a large community problem, there is a spirit at work. These spirits must be removed by the body of Christ.

There are spiritual forces operating over cities, nations, churches, schools, parks, and other locations. It is also important to identify how far-reaching the problem is to fight against it properly. Is the spirit local to a specific area? Is the spirit linked to a specific habit (watching porn, playing video games, taking drugs, and so on)? Demons and evil spirits often seek to enter our lives through our agreement with, or consumption of, ideas. These ideas are often linked to some form of action that is consistent with that agreement.

As a disclaimer, I would also say that, to some extent, every problem is a community problem. We must confess our sins to one another and repent to overcome any form of temptation. Any sin I commit while in the body of Christ has a direct impact on my brothers and sisters in the spiritual realm. I say this not so that we may judge or condemn a person or congregation, but to empower and love those we serve with while taking personal responsibility for our own lives. We do not wage war against flesh and blood (Ephesians 6:12); a person should never be condemned or targeted for their sins, because Jesus died for all our sins. Likewise, it is imperative that we always seek out intercessors when we need help; and we must also take responsibility for interceding for others. Prayer is not for a select group of people; rather, every member of the body must continually bring these things before the altar because we are a nation of priests (1 Peter 2:9). Intercession is required from all members of the body.

The third and last question asks whether there is an external source of fear when approaching this issue. It does not mean that we are afraid: It simply means that there is something stirring up apprehension inside us. This feeling is very common when we begin dealing with demons and malevolent spirits. It does not mean that we have anything to fear about the spirit: It means only that the enemy wants to distract us from God; to stop us having peace about His call on our lives to destroy the works of the enemy. As we grow, while fighting the enemy, our senses will be honed and we will no longer associate that feeling with fear; rather, it will simply mean it is time for battle.

These three questions are all things to consider and ask. The bottom line is that we are an army, and we move at the General's command. So, before you read further, I encourage you to ask God if this book is something you need now or whether it can wait. Does He want you to start this type of warfare or is there a more pressing personal need?

If you feel led to keep reading, I suggest you ask another two questions: "Who are the people that I have influence with or who influence me? Will they benefit from engaging with the ideas in this book?" This is not a path that anyone should ever take alone. We are one body; but if we are divided, we will fall.

For reflection

Here are some follow-up questions and activities for individuals or groups.

1. By reading this book, what are you looking for?
   - Should you be more focused on learning something specific or be more open in your approach?
2. Have there been times when you may have misdiagnosed a spiritual problem?
   - When that occurred, what was the solution?
3. How do you already think of spiritual warfare?
   - Are you open to hearing more or is your view rigid?
4. List some issues you believe are affecting your community.
   - Compare your list with those of others in your group.

CHAPTER 2

QUESTIONS: WHY THEY
MATTER

Socrates was an Ancient Greek philosopher who had a profound effect on the history of Western culture. His primary contribution was the process called the Socratic method: a form of discussion and argument based on asking questions to draw out critical thinking and biases. Questions and how they are phrased will generate all manner of different answers and, when used properly, are the single most powerful tool of reason any person can possess.

The historical importance of questions also exists within Scripture. The Jewish rabbis and Jewish culture have always prized asking questions and using critical thought to gain understanding. For example, this practice is found in classical rabbinical literature, which uses a dialog that incorporates asking and answering questions. This technique is also observed in the apostle Paul's writing and in the Old Testament.

What shall we say then? Are we to continue in sin that grace may abound? By no means! How can we who died to sin still live in it? Do you not know that all of us who have been baptized into Christ Jesus were baptized into his death? We were buried therefore with him by baptism into death, in order that, just as Christ was raised from the dead by the glory of the Father, we too might walk in newness of life.

(Romans 6:1–4)

This example shows how Paul uses questions to create a dialogue and preempt any criticism of his teachings.

Questions are also used in philosophy to build ideas. Simple questions such as "Who am I?" can lead to all kinds of new questions, such as "What defines a human?", "Am I a product of my past, my actions, circumstances, or a combination of the three?", and "To what extent are my actions a representation of me?" While there exist many answers to these questions, there is no conclusive answer. Rather, these questions help to develop understanding.

Questions exhibit immense power over our day-to-day life; and asking appropriate and relevant questions is necessary to engage with God as well as to live a healthy lifestyle. One of the greatest tricks the enemy can use against the church is to ask questions that hide lies. One might ask how can one lie by asking a question? The simple answer is to frame a question in a way that encourages a response based on false assumptions. An example of this is a question the Pharisees ask Jesus:

"Teacher, we know that you are true and do not care about anyone's opinion. For you are not swayed by appearances, but truly teach the way of God. Is it lawful to pay taxes to Caesar, or not? Should we pay them, or should we not?" But, knowing their hypocrisy, he said to them, "Why put me to the test? Bring me a denarius and let me look at it." And they brought one. And he said to them, "Whose likeness and inscription is this?" They said to him, "Caesar's." Jesus said to them, "Render to Caesar the things that are Caesar's, and to God the things that are God's." And they marveled at him.

(Mark 12:14–17)

If Christ had instead responded that they should give taxes to Caesar, they would have been able to sway the people against him; but if He had answered that taxes should not be paid to Caesar, then He could have been labeled a zealot whom they could have arrested. The question has a lie embedded in it: that the coin or currency is owned by the individual in whose hands it is rather than the nation-state or empire. The implication from Jesus' actual answer is that we, who are made in the image of God, owe to God what is His.

Another example of a question asked to undermine the truth occurs when Jesus is in the wilderness and is tempted by Satan. Satan says, "If you are the Son of God, command this stone to become bread" (Luke 4:3). This sentence is structured to force Jesus to ask Himself this question: "Am I the Son of God?" If Christ had focused on answering the question, He would have allowed the temptation of Satan to end His fast. It is because He chooses not to answer the question "Who do you say that you are?" that He does not fall prey to the lies of Satan. In fact, rather than just avoiding the question, He exposes the fallacy by pointing back to His Father in heaven (Matthew 4:4). Jesus doesn't defend His claim, nor does He ignore the accuser; He responds with the truth missing from the original question. If Christ is the Son of God, then He is defined by God's word and not His own word, as a man, in that moment.

When we are under attack by the demonic, most of the time it will be through lies in the form of questions, statements, commands, or feelings. If we engage with those lies, it gives the enemy a foothold that allows him to wreak havoc in our lives. Simple questions can often be the best response to these lies, as they quickly form a barrier between us and the enemy. Some good questions are "Where is this thought coming from?", "How can I apply Scripture, and which Bible passages should I examine?", and "What do I believe?" These questions are open (that is, they require more than a yes or no answer) and do not predetermine the type of answer.

Open questions do not require the asker to know the answer before it comes. Another example would be "What is your favorite memory from childhood?" This question allows the one who is asking to receive an answer for which they have no prior knowledge. This is important because it allows us to examine information outside our perspectives. Although this process does not guarantee an immediate response, it enables us to find honest answers, therefore potentially removing bias from the questions that are being asked. Posing honest, open questions is the only way to engage with the truth and to understand it. Likewise, not answering dishonest questions is equally important to prevent deception.

When engaging in spiritual warfare, we need to make sure that we are equipped with the "sword of the Spirit" (Ephesians 6:17; see also Hebrews 4:12), which is the word of God, so that we can address the enemy's antagonistic questions. The word of God equips us to strike down lies, and it leads us to the truth.

For the weapons of our warfare are not of the flesh but have divine power to destroy strongholds. We destroy arguments and every lofty opinion raised against the knowledge of God, and take every thought captive to obey Christ, being ready to punish every disobedience, when your obedience is complete.

(2 Corinthians 10: 4–6)

Questions are the bridge between the word of God and our personal thoughts. They allow us to apply the values rooted in a question to our thinking and belief; but they are also important for engaging with God and being led to victory over the enemy. For example, anyone approaching a home that has spiritual unrest should, first, pray for protection and, second, ask God what is responsible for the unrest. Each Christian needs to learn to discern the voice of God personally to be able to engage in warfare, for we know from Scripture that His "sheep hear [His] voice" (John 10:28).

Once you begin asking God questions, you must remain open to any answer: some responses may not seem to be answers when they are. For instance, God may begin to talk about a topic, rather than give a specific answer. This is important because that topic is often the spiritual solution to the problem. An example might be if we were to ask God about a way to ease depression; God might impress upon us the importance of praising His name. This may not at first seem relevant but, according to Scripture, the Lord wants "to give [us] ... the oil of gladness instead of mourning, the garment of praise instead of a faint spirit" (Isaiah 61:3). This verse indicates that the depression may be a product of spiritual warfare; or simply that the depressed person's spirit is faint because it has not been strengthened with praise. Later, I will go through some examples of ideas that the Bible offers to respond to specific spirits.

. . .

How to ask an effective question

Let's focus on developing the skill of asking questions. Here are three characteristics of good questions.

1. A good question does not assume an answer. For example, "What does love look like?" might be more helpful than "Why won't they love me?" The second question assumes a lack of love and that love should be expressed in a specific way.

2. A good question does not imply or assume a circumstance. For example, "Why does this always happen to me?" assumes that a situation always happens, or that the circumstance is destined to occur. On the other hand, a good question would be "Why is this a pattern in my life?" or "What led to this circumstance?"

3. A good question allows for answers that exist outside our current perspective. For example, "What is my next step?" and "If it is true that ... then how should my response change?" These questions are far superior to those that elicit simple yes or no answers, as they allow context and explanation.

For reflection

Practicing asking questions is something that it is necessary to do daily. So, before we continue, I have some questions for you. Remember that it's OK not to have an answer: it's more important to ask the question and to let yourself sit with it. Here are some questions to think about.

1. Which beliefs do you hold that are too sacred to question?
2. What do you say that you believe in but do not live out?
3. What do you personally hope to gain by reading this book?
4. What does the cross mean to you?
   - Why does it mean that to you?
   - Did it mean that to you yesterday?
   - Do you believe it will mean that to you tomorrow?
5. What is your favorite subject to talk to God about?
   - What is His favorite topic to share with you?
6. In Scripture, what do you disagree with or struggle to believe?
   - Have you brought this struggle to God and asked Him to explain it?
7. When you have hope, do you hope for a specific outcome or for a general change in circumstances?
   - What does it mean to have your hope anchored in Christ?
8. In 1 Corinthians 13:13, it says, "So now faith, hope, and love abide, these three; but the greatest of these is love."
   - Faith, hope, and love: which of these has the most to do with your personal walk with God?
   - Which one has the least to do with your personal walk with God?
   - How will discovering your answers to (a) and (b) change your personal walk with God?

CHAPTER 3

A DISCOURSE ON SPIRITS

It has occurred to me that perhaps you, the reader, may have an understanding of spirits different from the one in this book. Therefore, it might be best to define what a spirit is by focusing on the effect it has rather than its source or origin. So, each spirit may be defined by how it affects people or communities.

We in the Western world value rationality. We are therefore likely to have some skepticism about the existence of spirits. We might fail to believe that they are real because the concept of such beings is rarely described in a sensible and consistent way. Thoughts on this topic may conjure up an image of ghosts or specters. All manner of myths and stories paint too many pictures to capture and reconcile these ideas. So, to understand the essence of what Christians mean when we call something a "spirit" is important, both in the context of Scripture and for understanding the importance of how to respond to them.

When describing an individual, we might portray their physical appearance, their traits, their associates, their effect on the environment, or perhaps where they come from. When describing a spirit, we become very limited in our ability to build a complete description. A spirit has no physical body; nor can we reliably perceive its allies, or even its source or origin. Therefore, we define it by its characteristics and effects.

To begin, let's engage in a simple thought experiment. Imagine, if you would, an idea that compels a man to drink too much. The idea works like this: "I am in so much pain; the only way to survive is to numb myself with alcohol." This idea, when it is in accord with the man's will, begins to twist his actions. When, once, he could be sober and hold a steady job, he now finds that he is addicted to liquor, low on cash, and unemployed. His friends have left him, saying that they can't watch him kill himself. This man then sits in his apartment and continues to engage with the idea that tells him to drink because the pain is unbearable. He defends the idea by saying to himself that his friends have never understood him: If they knew the pain that he felt, they wouldn't judge him for drinking. He justifies his actions by thinking that he doesn't even drink as much as an acquaintance at a bar he frequents. In fact, he would very much rather be in that bar at this moment.

This man is held captive: The idea twists and turns in his mind like a parasite. He is consumed by believing a lie. He begins to define himself by his vice. He is no longer simply a man: He is a drunkard or a whiskey man. The problem is that this idea long ago stopped functioning as a normal thought. The moment he conceded to this belief—"I am in so much pain; the only way to survive is to numb myself with alcohol"—his life became one of bondage to this thought. We might define this as the effect of a spirit upon him: some Christians call these ideas "spirits." For certain ideas, when accepted, become parasitic and destroy people's lives: Spirits, by their very nature, interact with humans like "living ideas;" and, like ideas, they defend themselves like people who defend their egos. ("Ego" may be defined as a façade we use when protecting our pride.)

What then is the value or belief held that leads to this living idea? Well, one way to identify a living idea is by naming it as the feeling or consequence it seeks to reproduce. A living idea can produce fear: Christians would call such an idea a "spirit of fear." A raft of thoughts and beliefs that makes someone depressed and to feel a weight on their chest would be called a "spirit of heaviness." A "Leviathan spirit" would be a spirit that is tyrannical and prideful (based on a reading of Job 41:1–34). So, we often assign descriptions to spirits based on the traits they exhibit. Our minds can conjure up images of such spirits, but these are usually only how we *think* such entities should look.

Grasping this concept is all that is necessary to begin one's journey to understanding spiritual warfare. As we continue to experience or encounter these living ideas, we begin to see what people in ancient times consistently saw: Spirits defend and propagate themselves through speech and actions. Over time, ideas can seep into cultures and the minds of members of a community. They spread virally and can hold sway over nations. Take, for instance, the idea of communism: Think of how it seeks to reproduce itself and attempts to control everyone. Or think of the idea of humanism: Consider how it shifts the focus from the glory of God to the glory of man.

Now, some people can detect these ideas, whether through a spiritual gift or by being able to recognize a facial expression that is not quite right. They might pick up an indication that something is wrong, hidden in the way someone speaks. However, even if unnoticed by an observer, everyone is affected by ideas. How many times have we heard someone remark, "I can hear my mother saying ..." or how often does someone randomly begin singing a song that they heard once? The point is that not every thought that we have is our own. Whether the mind is affected by an idea, a memory, or an experience, it is often not as isolated a sanctuary as we might hope. For when we sit alone with our thoughts, we hear numerous voices, have lots of feelings, or see various images in our minds. Many of these experiences do not originate within us but, rather, can be external in nature.

I believe that this notion of spirits as living ideas is far more compatible with the Western psyche. The longer we live our lives, the more we begin to find that rational explanation fails to explain coincidences and events that often appear to be planned. Perhaps our human minds are seeking patterns around us. But that does not change how powerful ideas are when we give them belief. Belief and faith are key for these ideas to have power. Once believed, they will take ownership of us. Those possessed by such beliefs may even begin to stop seeming like themselves.

Now that we have a starting point for what spirits are, we can also understand something that is foundational to the concept of spiritual warfare: *We are not these ideas*. If we can point to their traits, recognizing that they are external, then we can understand them to be distinct from us. We can understand that a spirit wants to define us; but we can also know that the spirit is not who we are. People who understand this concept go from being addicts to those who have an addiction problem. They can go from being liars to those who struggle to be honest. Once we separate the spirit from the person, we can see the belief that binds them to it. Fear and faith are both forms of belief that bind us to these spirits. A man who is afraid of what others think may become a liar because he believes that other people's opinions define him. A man who believes his actions are unforgivable, or that his children have abandoned him, might believe that he needs to self-medicate, to drown his sorrows.

The problem here is that people who are tied to one of these spirits have no other way to define themselves. They can choose another spirit to believe in; but, still, they cannot define themselves. To be able to define themselves, individuals must have complete agency over their lives. People with the most commendable self-control still fail to control every aspect of their being. Any attempt at self-definition would lead to cognitive dissonance, as there would be parts of themselves that fall outside their definition. A simple example is that very few people have the ability to control their heartbeats; and even if they do, they have no control over them while sleeping. If there is no ability to exert control completely over the physical, it follows that there cannot be complete control over the mental or emotional as well, due to the interconnectedness of the systems. There will always be gaps in control, which is why I believe the Scriptures list self-control as part of the fruit of the Spirit (Galatians 5:22).

To attempt to control ourselves often results in partnering with a spirit of pride. We each understand our place in the world through our purpose. To strip someone of purpose leaves only belief in yet another spirit: nihilism. We cannot escape our need to be bound by these spirits: This aspect of our nature seems inexplicably tied to us through belief. This is why we, as Christians, must each be defined by Christ as a new creation. The idea that we can become the people we were made to be by a good and benevolent God gives us the freedom to live our lives in ways that honor us and others, without being presumptuous.

The Bible states:

For all who are led by the Spirit of God are sons of God. For you did not receive the spirit of slavery to fall back into fear, but you have received the Spirit of adoption as sons, by whom we cry, "Abba! Father!" The Spirit himself bears witness with our spirit that we are children of God.

(Romans 8:14–16)

Given this example, we see that we need to be led by a spirit; and Christ gave us the Holy Spirit that we might be able to follow Him. The Holy Spirit is the Spirit of God sent to mankind to guide us and to allow us to have union with God. One way the Bible describes the Holy Spirit is by listing His characteristics: "But the fruit of the Spirit is love, joy, peace, patience, kindness, goodness, faithfulness, gentleness, self-control; against such things there is no law" (Galatians 5:22–23).

With these things considered, it is plain to see why it is necessary to engage in spiritual warfare. Spirits that have a stronghold or are rooted in a community often have to be addressed before anyone can hear or see God. These spirits draw the attention of humanity in other directions, manipulating our beliefs, so that we cannot believe the truth of who Christ is or what kind of healing is available. Individuals who have committed violent acts may believe that they are too wicked and worthless to be loved by Christ; that they can hardly conceive of anyone wanting to spend time with them, let alone die for their transgressions. Those who steal may be so blinded by the fear of not having enough, or of never having the lives they hope for, that they are afraid to stop stealing, and instead invest in lives they hate.

Furthermore, communities can be manipulated by these beliefs. The members of a community may think that they are oppressed and downtrodden; that violence is the only path to freedom. When the spirit of hatred sets in, they become unable to see others as God made them. A church can be so possessed by gossip that it creates a community of manipulation and control, playing politics rather than producing the fruit of the Spirit; and its people justify their behavior as "venting." These community spirits have to be dealt with in a way that is different from managing personal trauma or individual fears. These beliefs exist within the community and therefore require community effort to end them.

For reflection

Before we continue, let's take some time to reflect to see if we can spot any lies that we believe. In other words, we must "first take the log out of [our] own [eyes]" (Matthew 7:5) so that we can see (and hear) what Christ is saying to us.

1. Which belief do you hold that prevents you from loving others?
2. Which fruit of the Spirit do you not consistently produce?
   - Is there a fear or a belief that prevents you from doing so?
3. How often are your thoughts focused on yourself (not simply on whether they are positive or negative)? For example, "I am ... wrong, not enough, stupid, great, influential," and so on. Alternatively, how often are your thoughts focused on what others think of you, what you are capable of, or on your experience of something? For example, "I just want them to like me" or "How can I ...?"
   - If you do think in these terms, what kind of thoughts do you have?
   - How can you frame those thoughts in a way that makes God the focus? For example, "God says I am ..." or "What must I surrender to Christ to ...?"
4. Do you believe anyone is beyond salvation? Why?
5. Did Christ love Judas less than His other disciples?
6. Is there anyone God doesn't want to be saved? Reflect on 2 Peter 3:9.

CHAPTER 4

THE SPIRIT OF HATRED AND THE STRATEGY OF FORGIVENESS

T he spirit of hatred is a force that has been plaguing humanity almost from the very beginning. It is first seen only four chapters into the Bible, in the story of Cain and Abel. This spirit has become so intertwined with our cultural development that it leaves us with this question: How do we stop it from moving in our communities?

First, we need to know what we are up against. Hatred is defined as an intense dislike or feeling of ill-will towards someone or something; but unfortunately, this definition does not highlight the truth of what this spirit is. To learn what it is, we can look at Scripture. The Bible says, "Everyone who hates his brother is a murderer" (1 John 3:15); and we know from Genesis 4 that Cain's hatred of Abel led to murder. The spirit of hatred is the spirit of murder: It knows that we are most likely to entertain evil thoughts when blinded by anger. In 1 John 2:11, it says, "But whoever hates his brother is in the darkness and walks in the darkness, and does not know where he is going, because the darkness has blinded his eyes." And anger that is not put to rest gives a place for this spirit to come to blind us: It is written, "Do not let the sun go down on your anger, and give no opportunity to the devil" (Ephesians 4:26–27). This point is important because, when we sleep, short-term memory becomes long-term memory, which means that anger can become bitterness overnight.

Hatred's mission is to distort how we see one another and to create division among all people. Evil spirits work to prevent us from seeing the truth of a matter. Hatred does so by compelling us to see other humans as enemies, stripping away their humanity, goodness, and virtues. When we partner with this spirit, we become unwilling to love someone, and we can no longer see that person as the image of God. This fact also makes it impossible to hear God's voice regarding that individual or any situation that involves them. The lens through which we see the world becomes the reality we live in. If we fall into such deep darkness, we may attempt to rationalize our hatred and justify it, thinking it reasonable, when we are actually cherry-picking truths. Hatred will then have more of a say in our decision-making than our own mental faculties will. For Christians, it is important not to let any belief hinder our ability to hear God's voice, to be vigilant in reading Scripture, and to discover the lies we believe about God and humanity.

First, let us look at the passage in Genesis, where hatred is first introduced in Scripture.

In the course of time Cain brought to the LORD an offering of the fruit of the ground, and Abel also brought of the firstborn of his flock and of their fat portions. And the LORD had regard for Abel and his offering, but for Cain and his offering he had no regard. So Cain was very angry, and his face fell.

(Genesis 4:3–5)

We see that the first fruits Cain withheld from God led God to acknowledge him according to his offering. This was in contrast to Abel, who brought the firstborn of his flock. God said to Cain:

Why are you angry, and why has your face fallen? If you do well, will you not be accepted?

(Genesis 4:6–7)

Instead of taking responsibility for his actions, Cain chose to dwell on his anger. In the very next verse, it becomes plain that, in Cain's heart, anger had given place to hatred and the desire to murder.

And when they were in the field, Cain rose up against his brother Abel and killed him. (Genesis 4:8)

This story illustrates the progression from anger to hatred; it finally concludes with a man who acts in agreement with the spirit of hatred. The spirit of hatred schemes, plots, plans, and continually repeats the offense in the mind of its victim. It uses the passionate response of hatred to create a negative judgment of the victim. This spirit is intentional and persistent, seeking to drive an individual into an obsessive state that blinds them to reality. It begins to shape and twist the way they view the world. Evidence of this belief becomes increasingly apparent with every passing moment, until all someone can do is be consumed with achieving destructive goals.

So how do we stop it? How, as leaders and influencers in our community, can we crush this enemy?

The strategy: Forgiveness

To find the answers to these questions, we need only read the story of Stephen in Acts. After Stephen gave a summary of Israel's Old Testament history to reveal who Jesus is, the Sanhedrin (the supreme Jewish council) responded in a way that exposed the spirit they served:

Now when they heard these things they were enraged, and they ground their teeth at him. But he, full of the Holy Spirit, gazed into heaven and saw the glory of God, and Jesus standing at the right hand of God. And he said, "Behold, I see the heavens opened, and the Son of Man standing at the right hand of God." But they cried out with a loud voice and stopped their ears and rushed together at him. Then they cast him out of the city and stoned him. And the witnesses laid down their garments at the feet of a young man named Saul. And as they were stoning Stephen, he called out, "Lord Jesus, receive my spirit." And falling to his knees he cried out with a loud voice, "Lord, do not hold this sin against them." And when he had said this, he fell asleep.

(Acts 7:54–60)

Here, again, we see hatred stirred up. This was a spirit that was already in the hearts of the council members. They had kindled their anger towards Christ and those who followed Christ, having already sent Jesus to His death. The rebuke that the biblical history (given by Stephen) dealt them stirred up their hatred, leading them to kill an innocent man.

Stephen, filled with the wisdom of the Holy Spirit, showed us how to break the power of the spirit of hatred: With his final breath, he forgave those killing him.

Although Stephen died, I believe that it was at this moment that God began breaking the hold of the spirit of hatred on Saul. Two chapters later, we read that when "Saul [was] still breathing threats and murder against the disciples of the Lord", he encountered a vision of Jesus, who told him to go into a city (Damascus) and who blinded him (Acts 9:1–8). Saul was now made to suffer physically the spiritual effects of hatred: blindness and darkness. He was told to go see a man named Ananias (whose name comes from the Hebrew word for "mercy"). It was only by the mercy of God, and by receiving His grace, that Saul was made to see again: "And immediately something like scales fell from his eyes, and he regained his sight" (Acts 9:18). It was the power of forgiveness that broke the spirit of hatred that was upon Saul. It gave him room for repentance and transformed him into one of the most influential leaders of the church.

The power of the spirit of hatred lies in its ability to blind and to encourage us to hold grudges and anger in view, thereby distorting our perspectives on others. Forgiveness produces compassion but hatred produces resentment; when people let go of grudges and anger, it becomes possible to see things accurately. It clearly follows that forgiveness renders the spirit of hatred powerless. Hatred plots while forgiveness shows mercy and extends grace. The cross broke the power of hatred and murder when Jesus forgave us for our transgressions.

You might ask, how does this apply practically to a church or group of Christians? Well, simply put, if the spirit of hatred comes against your home, church, or congregation, the best and most powerful solution is to forgive those who are operating in hatred. We forgive first, before the Father, and then follow through by extending grace to the community or individuals who are antagonizing us.

It is important to understand that the spirit of hatred craves death and murder. Therefore, a man who hates another man will sometimes feel this craving even when all he is doing is thinking about the man he hates. For anybody, hatred—if left unchecked and if the person is unrepentant—will lead to murder. Hating a political leader, hating a family member, even hating an organization will lead to murder. Even if that murder is imagined only in the heart, it is still murder. Frequently, fear of repercussions, honor, or strongly held beliefs may interrupt this spirit; but if these values are eroded, then this spirit can seize control. When the spirit is left unchecked, it will progress from encouraging obsession to prompting violence, abuse, and murder. The spirit of murder wants its victims to be trapped in anger and offense. At times, extending love and forgiveness may place people in harm's way, as it did Stephen. This is why it is so important to remember the gift we as Christians have: eternal life in Christ.

When Christ died on the cross, those of us who believe died with Him and were raised to life only through His grace, which now allows us to walk in the born-again life. Physical death or martyrdom is never without purpose as long as we actively pursue the voice of God for our specific situations. I also believe that God can spare us from death and resurrect our bodies. Therefore, it is important that we walk not in fear but in boldness, rejoicing not in earthly life but in the life that we have received from Christ and His sacrifice. If our minds are set on heavenly things and we are committed to doing His work, I believe the spirit of hatred will fail. I encourage you to seek God's word and will with regard to forgiving, and taking conciliatory action towards, communities or individuals infected with hatred. As long as we actively forgive them before the Father, we can put faith in what Scripture says:

If you forgive the sins of any, they are forgiven them; if you withhold forgiveness from any, it is withheld.

(John 20:23)

For reflection

Here are some questions and activities to help us to reflect on whether we unjustly judge others.

1. What are some examples of a belief or a perspective leading to an action?
2. What are some details that someone blinded by hatred fails to see when judging someone?
3. What are some details that you may have overlooked in the past, when holding a belief about someone?
    - How did you realize that you were missing some information?
4. Are there any ways in which you judge others from a place of unforgiveness?
5. Read 2 Corinthians 5:14–21.
    - How should we view other Christians?
    - How should we view non-Christians?
6. Any area of your life that is not aligned with Christ is an area in which a spirit can influence you. Take some time to pray. Ask God to show you whom you have unjustly judged so that you can repent of doing so.

CHAPTER 5

CHAPTER 5

THE SPIRIT OF LUST AND THE STRATEGY OF HUMILITY

Lust is another spirit that attempts to divide humanity through distorting our perceptions of one another. This spirit seeks to control our lives and force us into a continual struggle with our own desires. It uses our desires to cloud our views of others, causing us to see them as a means to an end. If this spirit binds itself to our legitimate desires, then we need to find a way to separate desire from lust.

Let us move toward a better understanding of lust. A good definition of lust is *the unrestrained pursuit of the desires of the flesh*. As such, it is not limited to sexual desire but means any desire that is unfettered: Desire for power, desire for pleasure, desire for experience, and desire for status can all be forms of lust. Temptation starts with desire. James 1:14 says, "But each person is tempted when he is lured and enticed by his own desire." Also, the apostle Peter wrote, "Beloved, I urge you as sojourners and exiles to abstain from the passions of the flesh" (1 Peter 2:11). This example is one of many where the Bible specifically addresses the "passions of the flesh" or lusts of the world. The impact of indulging in lust was a major concern for the early church.

Now, if we understand that our own desires can provide a foothold for lust, then we can understand why this spirit is so efficient at tormenting its victims. In the Bible, we see many passages about lust: Some give examples of those who fought and won against the spirit, while others are stories of those who succumbed to the desires of the flesh. An example of lust is illustrated early in the book of Genesis:

So when the woman *saw* that the tree was good for food, and that it was a delight to the eyes, and that the tree was to be desired to make one wise, she took of its fruit and ate.
(Genesis 3:6; emphasis added)

In this passage, we see many sins manifest; but specifically, I would like to highlight the very first portion, where it says, "the woman saw it was good for food." Here, seeing opens the door to lust; it is an acknowledgement of the desire of the flesh on which the woman subsequently acts. And in this verse, we discover the very first clue about how to respond to lust: This spirit depends on how and what we see.

The word "saw" in Genesis 3:6 is translated from the Hebrew word *râ'âh*. This is a root word that means "to see;" it has a connotation implying to see physically outside oneself. And it can be applied to mean seeing both literally and figuratively. In this case, we can conclude that the woman had already seen the fruit physically; so *râ'âh* reveals a change in her perspective, which followed from the conversation with the serpent. To begin with, her viewpoint was based on the rule that God had given: "But of the tree of the knowledge of good and evil you shall not eat" (Genesis 2:17). But, after talking to the serpent, her perspective began to change and she saw the fruit as something accessible—edible; then she started to desire it as a delicacy.

Lust wants to control how we see the world and will therefore try to twist our perspective through the lens of desire. This spirit also wants us to accept *its* desire as our own, thereby making any indulgence a manifestation of our identity. This is a sinister trick because people afflicted by this spirit are being fed the spirit's desires, not their own. This is often why, when individuals give themselves over to lust, they frequently become increasingly wicked. The desire of this spirit is to corrupt and destroy its victims through moral and mental erosion. Its goal is accomplished once its targets have completely abandoned themselves to their own depraved hunger.

Now, let's look at passages that show what success and failure might look like when battling lust.

. . .

Now Joseph was handsome in form and appearance. And after a time his master's wife cast her eyes on Joseph and said, "Lie with me." But he refused and said to his master's wife, "Behold, because of me my master has no concern about anything in the house, and he has put everything that he has in my charge. He is not greater in this house than I am, nor has he kept back anything from me except you, because you are his wife. How then can I do this great wickedness and sin against God?"

(Genesis 39:6–9)

This passage begins with describing Joseph's appearance: The implication is that someone saw him and, we as readers, need to understand the context of what was seen. Verse 7 goes on to explore how the wife of Potiphar looked at him and decided that he was of value to her flesh. The spirit of lust had already gripped her and was twisting her desire into an unrestrained pursuit of Joseph. She saw; she engaged; and then she pursued.

Joseph also saw Potiphar's wife physically; but we do not have a description of her appearance. The lack of a description does not mean that she was unattractive; rather, it implies that her appearance was not relevant to Joseph or, indeed, the reader. The reader does not need to know because what Joseph said gives us a greater insight into his perspective. Joseph understood his place and purpose, which had more value to him than his fleshly desires. In fact, the only argument he offered for declining Potiphar's wife's advances was his relationship with, and respect for, his master, about whom he said, "He is not greater in this house than I am." Joseph never acknowledged Potiphar as anything less than his master. This is the key to facing lust: The required responses are humility and the valuing of others as more important than we are.

The strategy: Humility

Lust has no power when desire is restrained or kept in check by a greater value or priority, such as having a true perspective of our own status: humility. Humility is not thinking that others are greater than they are; rather, it is choosing to view others, and walk and talk, as people who know our true position and responsibility. While false humility demeans us, real humility allows us to walk boldly and take the lower seat because our relationships and status are dependent on God.

Humility is relational: It means that we consider the needs of others before considering our own. Humility breaks the power of lust before and after we engage with it. Repentance from indulgence, and a healthy view of our place with respect to others, will keep our eyes off fleshly desires. Such a stance includes viewing someone according to God's plan and purpose, rather than according to their actions or their flesh.

In Genesis 39, Joseph understood clearly that the woman who spoke to him was not his own wife and, moreover, that she was the wife of his master. Instead of pointing to his "purity" and stating how he would not lie with her because they were not married, he pointed only to his relationship with his master, and how his master had given him authority and access to everything in the house except her. He did not acknowledge any scenario where he would be able to lie with her; nor did he depend on his own ability to restrain himself. He knew that acknowledging his relationship with his master was the only appropriate way to respond to lust. Purity, while of value in helping us to abstain from lust, is incapable of stopping the spirit of lust.

The spirit of lust taunts the pure and creates the illusion that the desire they feel is their own. This leads those who are pure to believe that they have done something wrong and have not protected their hearts, when in fact the thoughts and feelings that they experience were never their own. Earlier, we read James 1:14; let's now read it again, with verse 15: "Each person is tempted when he is lured and enticed by his own desire. Then desire when it has conceived gives birth to sin, and sin when it is fully grown brings forth death." There are times when the desires of the enemy are disguised to look similar to our own. If we claim ownership of the tainted desires as we feel them—rather than looking to our master, Christ, and our status in relation to others—we let sin enter in.

Not every thought in our heads is our own, and neither is every emotional response. We, as humans, know this to be true even though our gut reaction is to reject the idea when we hear it. Ideas bombard us daily through words, emotions (often through art that expresses or provokes a specific feeling), and images that can slowly seep into our minds. Therefore, choosing carefully what we listen to or watch is so important. For example, there is some music I can't listen to now because it communicates so strongly a message of lust: It is almost guaranteed to encourage me to fall into sin. As such, each person's triggers for these desires are different and it is important to watch how we respond in different situations.

Let's look at another passage that shows the pattern of the spirit of lust:

It happened, late one afternoon, when David arose from his couch and was walking on the roof of the king's house, that he saw from the roof a woman bathing; and the woman was very beautiful. And David sent and inquired about the woman. And one said, "Is not this Bathsheba, the daughter of Eliam, the wife of Uriah the Hittite?" So David sent messengers and took her, and she came to him, and he lay with her. (Now she had been purifying herself from her uncleanness.) Then she returned to her house.

(2 Samuel 11:2–4)

These verses reveal a few interesting points about how lust seeks to engage with individuals. At the start of the passage, we are told what King David sees. His physical sense of sight shows him something that he translates into a desire. He engages with his desire by inquiring about the woman on the roof. He then pursues her by sending a messenger to bring her to him. A small portion of the passage gives context: The woman was purifying herself from uncleanness. This is interesting because it shows that lust often preys upon the unclean and the vulnerable: Bathsheba was cleansing herself while exposed on a roof. Lust does not consider the state a person is in when it seeks to pursue them. There is no consideration from, or restraint by, lust about when to engage in immoral behavior. Had David considered the vulnerability of Bathsheba and placed a higher value on her safety and worth as a person, he would have been unable to use her as a means to an end.

Humility is not only about an understanding of status; it is also an attitude that helps us to view others with respect and as having value.

When we prize our friends, we cannot conceive of using them for our own desires, whether those desires are to dominate or to gain sexual pleasure. Someone who sees women for the worth they have as individuals will be less inclined to the temptation to use them. For men, a healthy perspective is to respect women and to acknowledge their value as human beings, which will allow wholesome relationships and friendships to flourish between the sexes. Likewise for women, the temptation can be to view men as a way of fulfilling a fantasy or desire. Such an attitude can at times prevent women from seeing men for who they are. When members of either sex do not cultivate humility, they are liable to see one another as a means to an end.

Without acknowledging the value of others, we have no guidelines on how to interact with people we are attracted to. However, we should recognize that this truth is not dependent on which gender we are drawn to; it can be extended to include any type of sexual desire. Any desire that is pursued can become an open door to lust if we don't view others as God created them. As a man, it is my deep love for my male friends that keeps me from ever entertaining the idea of using any man for sex. The other thing I take into consideration is knowing that, even if I were attracted to men, my God asks me to exercise restraint and to focus my desires on Him and His plan for my life. Therefore, it is humility that controls my sexual impulses, not my desires, wherever they may draw me. Likewise, valuing women causes my heart to seek relationships with them that honor and protect them. This is humbling because I must view women as more valuable than my own desires. I say this because, although I am not perfect, I know my place in the world with respect to God and humanity. When I lose sight of this, I become susceptible to lust and temptation.

To gain a perspective on biblical humility, let's look at a passage from Philippians:

Do nothing from selfish ambition or conceit, but in humility count others more significant than yourselves. Let each of you look not only to his own interests, but also to the interests of others. Have this mind among yourselves, which is yours in Christ Jesus.

(Philippians 2:3–5)

· · ·

In humility, we count others as more significant and we see that their interests are met first. It is important to acknowledge that we do not neglect or reject our own needs; but, rather, we admit that we have them. In short, this means that we act on our own desires only after we have understood and accepted what our responsibilities towards others are and have honored them. For example, when someone enters my house, I (as the host) must first make sure that everyone else has food before I can rest and enjoy my cooking.

Humility not only prevents lust from acting on our hearts; it can also help to keep it from entering our communities. Lust starts with our entertaining the desires of the flesh. The problem is that many desires of the flesh are misrepresented in society and through our own imperfect perspectives. Desires can often be confused with needs, so it is important to know the difference between a need and a desire before addressing either one. A need for human touch and compassion could be misinterpreted as a desire for sex, when the actual need itself is not sexual in nature. A need for food might be misrepresented as a desire for overindulgence and delicacies. Likewise, a need for security and safety may be taken as a desire for power. Often, when we look to others' needs first, we find that God is faithful to meet our own needs. The flesh is like an immature child who knows the pain of hunger but does not know how to satisfy it in a healthy manner. Dealing with needs and desires must be viewed in the context of Philippians 2:5: We have the capacity and capability to look after one another because of Christ within us. I am capable of recognizing needs when I resolve to bear in mind Christ's thoughts and actions. I am capable of meeting needs while I remain in Christ, as He strengthens me and empowers me to serve.

Lastly, I want to focus on what this means for those of us who are in Christ,

who, though he was in the form of God, did not count equality with God a thing to be grasped, but emptied himself, by taking the form of a servant, being born in the likeness of men. And being found in human form, he humbled himself by becoming obedient to the point of death, even death on a cross.

(Philippians 2:6–8)

· · ·

We look towards our Savior, who believed that service to others and meeting the needs of others were worth dying for. In His obedience to God, He emptied Himself and became a man who would die for the trespasses and lusts of humanity. Therefore, we ought to humble ourselves and, while doing so, separate ourselves from the spirit of lust, choosing instead to meet the needs of the body of Christ and the lost. Likewise, we as Christians can fulfill Romans 12:1-2 by presenting ourselves as living sacrifices to God. My interpretation of this is that giving my body as a sacrifice and renewing my mind requires me to give all that I am and have to God, and to burn it on the altar for His sake. I put the responsibility on God, therefore, to create new desires in me so that, through my submission, I become an expression of relationship with God in a way that I could not if I were to pursue my desires in my own strength. If Christ died to give me everything He lived for and earned, then it's my responsibility to give Him nothing less than everything. This includes my fears, my hopes, my dreams, my ambition, my family, my relationships, and my identity. Everything I have becomes part of my living sacrifice. What I receive in return is incomparable with what I sacrifice to God.

For reflection

These questions will help us to explore whether there is lust in our own lives and, if so, how to deal with it.

1. Was there a time when your desire had an impact on someone else?
   - If so, have you repented? What have you done to ensure that it never happens again?
2. What are some of the ways in which you can support those who struggle with lust?
   - What lies might they believe about themselves that could drive them to lust?
3. What details do people miss when engaging in thoughts of lust towards a person?
4. What is the relationship between sexual lust and modesty?
   - How necessary is modesty?
   - What are some things that might help or harm fellow brothers and sisters struggling with lust?
   - Are we responsible for responding to someone else's "weakness?" (See Genesis 4:9.) Why?
5. In what way does the spirit of lust subvert purity?
6. Has a thought ever run through your mind about something someone else said?
   - To what extent is this thought yours? To what extent is it someone else's?
   - Did you take ownership of the thought or reject it?
   - Was this choice active or passive?

CHAPTER 6

THE SPIRIT OF WITCHCRAFT AND THE STRATEGY OF THE FEAR OF THE LORD

It seems only fitting to address the spirit of witchcraft after the spirit of lust due to their tendency to work together. When this spirit is mentioned in church, people often quote the phrase "For rebellion is as the sin of witchcraft" (1 Samuel 15:23, NKJV). Personally, I view this as a mistake unless it is explained why rebellion is like witchcraft. Without addressing against whom we are rebelling and how, witchcraft can find its way into everyday life.

So, what is witchcraft? Is it summoning demons, divination, the casting of spells, or rituals? Is it rebellion? Is it those ancient practices that humanity uses to try to manipulate nature? To understand witchcraft, it is necessary to understand first the order on which creation is established. All creation was made by God; and it was made to exist in perfect order, with a perfect set of laws. (After all, how can anyone rebel if there are no laws?) All creation was made to exist within those laws and within the boundary of God's will.

Within this created order, universal spiritual laws determine how the universe, including the spiritual realm, functions. For something (or someone) to deviate from its intended purpose is both rebellion and an attempt to manipulate the spiritual order or break the laws for its own purposes. With this in mind, we can define the pursuit of one's own desires, outside the will of God, as witchcraft. Witchcraft is any behavior resulting from a desire that is contrary to the will of God; a desire that leads to spiritual practices designed to try to manipulate universal spiritual laws, such as the principle of reaping and sowing. Witchcraft is fueled by faith: a faith in manifesting one's own will on earth. This definition covers many practices, all of which can be called witchcraft.

Witchcraft is the practice of manifesting desires with intent. For example, a man believes that he will have a nice car one day. He works for that car and finds and buys one at a good price; the car is a reward for his labor. His striving for the car in this natural way is not rebellion. His belief about having the car is rooted in his desire; but he is not trying to overcome the barriers to his goal by force of will or spiritual manipulation. His longing for a nice car may be selfish or idolatrous, but it is not witchcraft. By contrast, a man who sits and practices visualization to receive a vehicle, without working for it, is practicing witchcraft. He is trying to overthrow reality to achieve his own goal; he is using one spiritual principle to subvert others.

Before going further on this topic, it is worthwhile examining a common practice within the church. The word of faith movement originated with believing in the will of God to receive what is prayed for. Initially, the focus was entirely on healing and taking care of others' needs. In recent decades, however, the word of faith movement has given birth to a heresy known as the prosperity gospel, which removes God's will from the equation in favor of adherents manifesting their own will. This is witchcraft. While it is important to be bold in our prayers and to recognize the authority of the Christian over demons and illness, it is evil to do so while neglecting the pursuit of God and His will. Whether it's God's will for me to grow wealthy or to be martyred, I nevertheless desire His will: When someone declares Jesus is Lord, they are surrendering their life to a master. Jesus is Lord. For us to move from heresy into righteousness, we must seek first the kingdom: as it is written, "This is the confidence that we have toward him, that if we ask anything according to his will he hears us" (1 John 5:14).

To manifest desires, it is necessary to understand spiritual laws and their application to manipulate them. The knowledge and understanding of these laws might be defined as a form of earthly wisdom. "This is not the wisdom that comes down from above, but is earthly, unspiritual, demonic. For where jealousy and selfish ambition exist, there will be disorder and every vile practice" (James 3:15–16). This wisdom, when accumulated, can be used to fulfill personal desires on earth. The distinction between witchcraft and lust comes when someone manipulates spiritual laws, rather than using physical means, to achieve certain goals. Because we covet wealth, we may achieve it through hard work, without resorting to witchcraft. But by following our lusts to fulfill our desires, we may also choose to manipulate people and situations through supernatural means. For example, it is common for people to seek fortune tellers and mediums to gain an edge in the world.

It is important to understand that these practices are still around today (even though many practitioners are charlatans) because they work. People return to them because what they produce is perceived as valuable. These days, Christians cannot afford to be ignorant about witchcraft because it is becoming increasingly prevalent. Churches that are ignorant of spiritual truths and realities often fail to address the breadth of occult experience that many young people have had and will continue to have. If we do not believe in demons, we are unable to explain how the demonic realm is using devices, such as Ouija boards, to ensnare and manipulate people. The Bible speaks to this topic: "The coming of the lawless one is by the activity of Satan with all power and false signs and wonders" (2 Thessalonians 2:9).

Faith is the currency of the spiritual realm; it is used to focus desires on a specific outcome and to change circumstances to achieve that outcome. Faith, or belief, works like a force supernaturally; when we believe, we give substance to our hopes (Hebrews 11:1). Willpower is exerted to control circumstances or achieve a certain outcome. For those who understand physics, this is like potential and kinetic energy. When a ball is held up high, it has the energy stored in it to fall when released: the stored energy is called potential energy. Faith is like potential energy. Willpower, on the other hand, is like the energy that is released when the ball falls, known as kinetic energy. This is why when someone believes something, actions or works are produced. Faith and works cannot be separated: Works are the manifestation of belief. The outworking of salvation is that, if we are saved by faith, then the works we produce will be rooted in belief in something true, rather than in a false belief or fear. For instance, two men may both give to charity: one out of fear for his reputation and one because he wants others to be cared for. The true value of the gift is determined by the belief and the intention. "All the ways of a man are pure in his own eyes, but the LORD weighs the spirit" (Proverbs 16:2).

Those who are not in submission to God must cultivate belief in an outcome because, otherwise, there is no way for them to exert control to change any situation. If a person trusts in a spiritual principle or an idea, they will align their life and actions with their own belief in that reality. This can result in a self-fulfilling prophecy: when someone believes something so strongly that their actions bring about that circumstance. This is why the Bible puts so much emphasis on belief. If I believe that I am a sinner, then I submit to that belief and fall into sin. If I believe that I am made righteous through Christ, I look for opportunities to grow in relationship with God and to display His goodness. Failing at something, while believing that He made me righteous, is an opportunity to repent and grow. After all, if sin is lawlessness (1 John 3:4), then Christians live their lives in submission to the law of Christ through repentance.

Therefore, for witchcraft to occur, faith and earthly wisdom regarding spiritual practices must be present: faith is required to manifest willpower; and earthly wisdom is required to manipulate spiritual laws. The New Testament letter of James relates how the wisdom of the world progresses to an end that is "demonic." This wisdom leads to selfishness and lust, which in turn create a demonic manifestation of personal will. This is contrary to the will of God and is a rebellion against God's intention for creation.

The power behind witchcraft is real; but it is a sad counterfeit of the Holy Spirit's power. After all, God created the universe and everything in it; demons, while manifesting evil by their own wicked will, exist only at the whim of God; they will be brought to an end. This is why wisdom from above is very different than wisdom from below: it is not rooted in selfishness but in God's will. "But the wisdom from above is first pure, then peaceable, gentle, open to reason, full of mercy and good fruits, impartial and sincere" (James 3:17). The manifestation of godly wisdom is rooted in humility; and it is focused on the benevolent God. The only thing that wisdom from above can produce is fruit according to the will of God.

Many Christians are not aware of what it means to have resurrection power living inside them (Romans 8:11); God, being the source of power, has no limitation. His power is given as a free gift because of the price paid by Jesus. Faith in God and His will make it possible to manifest the will of God on earth. Manifesting the will of God requires both wisdom rooted in His will for the world and faith that He is who He says He is.

Before discussing how to deal with the spirit of witchcraft in a community, it is pertinent to explain its limitations so that the church will not remain ignorant of the difference between the Holy Spirit and this spirit. First, in every occult practice, a necessary payment must be offered to compel the power to move. Payment might be in the form of sacrifice and rituals; but it can also be generated by making deals with demons. Often the price paid is greater than the value of the desired result, but the degree of this difference is dependent on the type of occult practice. Some rituals are less expensive than others. For a pricey ritual, the cost may be a seven-to-one ratio of sacrifice to desired outcome. For example, if a farmer wants to destroy a rival's crops using occult means, the cost to do so would be equivalent to seven times the crops' value. Cheaper methods are usually provided nearer to a one-to-one ratio, although they often require a lot more time and effort to perform. When seeking the help of the God of the Bible, Christians need only ask: God's power is absolute; so much so, that, when opposing the priests of Baal, Elijah delighted in mocking their false god (demon):

And they took the bull that was given them, and they prepared it and called upon the name of Baal from morning until noon, saying, "O Baal, answer us!" But there was no voice, and no one answered. And they limped around the altar that they had made. And at noon Elijah mocked them, saying, "Cry aloud, for he is a god. Either he is musing, or he is relieving himself, or he is on a journey, or perhaps he is asleep and must be awakened." And they cried aloud and cut themselves after their custom with swords and lances, until the blood gushed out upon them. And as midday passed, they raved on until the time of the offering of the oblation, but there was no voice. No one answered; no one paid attention.

(1 Kings 18:26–29)

Christians serve the living God and ought not to be impressed when encountering spirits incapable of offering anything of lasting value.

Compared to God, all other spirits are weak. Therefore, it is of far more benefit to represent God and to be obedient to His will, engaging in spiritual warfare only when led to do so. After mocking the ineffectualness of Baal, Elijah prays and asks God to show up (1 Kings 18:36–38). The primary difference between Elijah and the priests of Baal is that Elijah is not acting in accordance with his own will but with the will of God; and it is God's desire (no one else's) to release His power. God's love for His people compels the Holy Spirit to move in power through His children. It is why Christians are instructed to let love and compassion inform their actions.

Witchcraft, like most belief systems, depends on acts of faith. But that faith is being used to barter with entities that oppose God. In fact, demonic beings are incapable of manifesting any significant power on earth unless they are fueled by human belief. Fear is the most common form of belief that animates these demons (a fear of death, for example, is a belief that death has power over me); but they can also use devotion. A demon's power is dependent on the number of people who believe in it; therefore, demons over regions tend to be more powerful than demons that oppress individuals. While God has no limit to His power, He respects the free will of humanity and desires that we partner with His intervention through prayer and intercession. Even one or two intercessors can completely disrupt the power of the enemy in a place; often, though, overcoming spirits with larger territory requires a greater collective response from believers. This is because the primary battlefield of the spiritual realm is the minds and hearts of people. Spiritual warfare should be done in groups so that people can cover one another's weaknesses "and so fulfill the law of Christ" (Galatians 6:2). We should never undertake it alone.

Christians cannot perform rituals to convince God to move; rather, we partner with Him through expressions of devotion towards Him, such as praise, worship, shouting, clapping, dancing, repentance, prayer, submission, and prophetic acts. Biblical examples of prophetic acts include Moses striking the rock (Numbers 20:11), Namaan bathing in the Jordan (2 Kings 5:1–17), and Joshua building an altar of stones as a memorial (Joshua 4:1–7); any action that is directed by the Holy Spirit outside normal religious practice is a prophetic act. As for more expressive forms of worship, the original Hebrew terms for praise and worship include clapping, shouting, and even spinning around with violent emotion. In fact, during spiritual warfare, spending a significant amount of time proclaiming our love for God and our trust in Him is more potent than focusing on the enemy. We need to know only enough information to be obedient to the Lord of Hosts. Scripture says, "Yet [God is] holy, enthroned on the praises of Israel" (Psalm 22:3) and "God shall arise, his enemies shall be scattered" (Psalm 68:1). For God to destroy His enemies, it is simply enough for Him to show up.

How can we identify witchcraft from other spirits? As we have seen, this spirit is fueled directly through belief and earthly wisdom, leading it to have some common manifestations. The marks of witchcraft are stated in James 3:16: "For where jealousy and selfish ambition exist, there will be disorder and every vile practice." First, a common (and often the most obvious) sign of witchcraft is confusion or disorder. The spirit of witchcraft is manipulative in nature, so it attempts to create an environment that will cause people to change their behavior. Inciting selfish ambition and causing confusion are the two primary ways that this spirit does so. The Old Testament story of King Ahab of Israel and his wife Jezebel illustrates the work of this spirit:

And Ahab the son of Omri did evil in the sight of the Lord, more than all who were before him. And as if it had been a light thing for him to walk in the sins of Jeroboam the son of Nebat, he took for his wife Jezebel the daughter of Ethbaal king of the Sidonians, and went and served Baal and worshiped him.

(1 Kings 16:30–31)

In this passage, we see two factors concerning Ahab: He is seeking to fulfill his own desires, and he is drawn to Jezebel. A consequence of his behavior is his worshiping a new god. So, he has obviously rebelled against God's will; but Ahab compounds his wickedness by doing nothing to stop Jezebel from killing the prophets of the Lord (1 Kings 18:4). This crucial detail displays one of the key goals of this spirit: The first thing it attempts to do is silence the voice of God; then confusion becomes rampant and deception blinds people's minds, which is why some of the first signs of this spirit are a sense of confusion and difficulty in engaging in worship.

Selfish ambition and envy are also key aspects that identify the presence of this spirit. When jealousy exists or a desire to have what another possesses (envy), lust may drive someone to pursue the desires of their flesh. Selfishness and lust are the most common precursors to engaging in witchcraft and will always be present in the hearts of those who practice it. Often, this spirit will attempt to promote division in a church by fanning the flames of envy and selfishness in believers' hearts. A consequence can be rumors and gossip, hurting believers and causing them to turn against one another. Under such circumstances, church members begin to function like witches. By indulging in back-biting and slander, rooted in their own selfish beliefs, these people abandon submission to God in favor of pursuing their own desires. A common way this spirit enters the church is through a witch or a person who is led by demonic forces, potentially unknowingly; they begin to stir up strife and enmity, causing cliques and divisions to form. By doing so, an atmosphere of condemnation and confusion is created that allows the witch or demonized person to exert a level of influence over a group of people.

In 1 Kings 21:1–12, the elements of gossip, deception and manipulation are present when Jezebel sets in motion a scheme to falsely accuse (and ultimately have killed) the owner of a vineyard that Ahab covets. Witches and people who practice occult rituals often believe infiltration and manipulation to be valid tactics to manifest their desires. Sometimes this spirit will attempt to manipulate Christians into spreading chaos that eventually divides or destroys a congregation. This highlights why repentance is necessary if anyone has anything against a brother before making an offering to God (Matthew 5:23–24).

There are many resources that address this topic; some provide far more detail than I have here. If you believe that you might need more information for your situation, it may be wise to ask God whether you require resources in addition to this book. There is, however, a simple strategy that will weaken and uproot this spirit from a congregation of believers or a city.

The strategy: The fear of the Lord

It is easy enough to understand that witchcraft, being a type of rebellion, is solved through submission to God and repentance from selfish ambition. Entering into submission requires being led by the Holy Spirit. The fear of the Lord—knowing that God is perfect and committing to see His perfect will done—helps to correct false perspectives. Cultivating the fear of the Lord is necessary to prevent the movement and work of the spirit of witchcraft. Scripture teaches that the fear of the Lord leads to wisdom and knowledge: "The fear of the LORD is the beginning of wisdom" (Proverbs 9:10) and "The fear of the LORD is the beginning of knowledge" (Proverbs 1:7). Again, in Psalm 111:10, we see that the "fear of the LORD is the beginning of wisdom; all those who practice it have a good understanding. His praise endures forever!" To deal with the lies and confusion engendered by witchcraft, first fear the Lord and His commandments.

This fear is not a dread of punishment; rather, it is a holy fear rooted in an understanding of the vast difference between humanity and our perfect God.

And do not fear those who kill the body but cannot kill the soul. Rather fear him who can destroy both soul and body in hell.
(Matthew 10:28)

The fear of the Lord is an acknowledgment not only of the power but also of the authority and justice of the will of God. It is the most important aspect of walking free from witchcraft. We learn to fear the Lord by meditating on God's law and understanding that it is perfect because He is perfect, just as the psalmist did:

My tongue will sing of your word,
for all your commandments are right.
(Psalm 119:172)

Oh how I love your law!
It is my meditation all the day.
Your commandment makes me wiser than my enemies,
for it is ever with me.
I have more understanding than all my teachers,
for your testimonies are my meditation.
I understand more than the aged,
for I keep your precepts.

> I hold back my feet from every evil way,
> in order to keep your word.
> (Psalm 119:97–101)

God's commandments make us wiser because they lead us to fear Him as a just and mighty God. He allows us to receive the perfect judgment of mercy through the death of His Son on the cross: The judgment of God towards humanity is mercy through the blood of His Son.

If we have no fear of God and do not understand that His law is perfect, we become our own gods, determining right and wrong for ourselves (Romans 2:14). This is how selfishness and lust take root and lead us to pursue our own desires by any means possible. However, someone who believes in the perfect will of God seeks to manifest God's will even at the cost of their own life (Matthew 16:24). Unless churches cultivate a fear of the Lord that leads people to repentance, they will find that the perfect word of God is missing. The fear of the Lord is required to prophesy and to worship Him in truth. How can we worship God in truth if we do not know God as a perfect judge? How can we speak the word of God without compromise if, in our hearts, we question the validity of His words?

Imagine, if you will, a son who is disciplined by his loving father. That son is filled with fear of his father, not because he believes that his father will kill him but, rather, because he does not want to dishonor or disappoint his father. The son who loves the father doesn't fear punishment; he fears the loss of connection to and respect from his father. This type of fear is possible only when we know who our Father is. If we do not know that God is just and perfect, we have no fear of misrepresenting Him. Yes, we receive the love of our Father, and it makes us bold, but we also fear our Father, which keeps us in His will.

This is not to encourage us to ignore any questions or concerns we have about the Bible: It is to affirm the need for faith in who God is. We can ask Him questions and bring to Him any concerns we have about His actions; but we believe in His goodness. Children of God are not mindless; it is normal to have reservations when viewing the actions of a perfect being through a lens that is limited and finite. Christians ask questions in humility, not seeking to dispose of God or His law but to understand His law and will. For Christians, Christ is the fulfillment and manifestation of God's law; and having the indwelling Holy Spirit is the only way we can live perfect lives. Confidence that God is good and faith that God is just can be found through the fear of the Lord. There is nowhere this is summed up better than in Job:

I know that you can do all things,
    and that no purpose of yours can be thwarted.
    "Who is this that hides counsel without knowledge?"
    Therefore, I have uttered what I did not understand,
    things too wonderful for me, which I did not know.
    "Hear, and I will speak;
    I will question you, and you make it known to me."
    I had heard of you by the hearing of the ear,
    but now my eye sees you;
    therefore I despise myself
    and repent in dust and ashes.
    (Job 42:2–6)

For reflection

Here are some questions to help us to consider God's perfection and our vulnerability to manipulative behaviors.

1. Have you ever partnered with selfishness and judged a brother or sister in Christ?
   - What have you put in place to ensure you do not fall back into that sin?
2. What are some core beliefs that lead to selfishness?
3. A curse is speaking badly about someone.
   - Have you ever cursed someone?
   - Are you willing to revoke that curse and bless that person instead?
4. How can we become unknowing participants in demonic schemes?
5. For you, what does it look like to fear the Lord?
6. Regarding God's love or perfection, is there any belief you can think of that might hold you back from fearing him?
7. Are there some activities you can practice in groups of two or three that help to display devotion and submission to God? It's OK to be creative.

CHAPTER 7

THE SPIRIT OF JEALOUSY AND THE STRATEGY OF CELEBRATION

At this point, it seems appropriate to continue exploring and addressing spirits that manipulate men and women through desire. Therefore, we will look at the spirit of jealousy. Like the spirit of lust, the spirit of jealousy occurs in the story of Joseph. This spirit attempts to blind its victims by using comparisons. It is important to separate jealousy from envy: both are often mistakenly used interchangeably. While similar, envy is focused on desire for an object, whereas jealousy affects relationships between people. Jealousy does not want what others have because of a desire for those things; rather, it cultivates the desire to keep others from certain personal interactions or objects. Another way to define these two would be to say envy desires a thing, and jealousy seeks to deprive someone of the thing. Jealousy is simpler than greed or envy in many ways. Jealousy says, "I fear that they will take what I deserve." In fact, when jealousy is tied to an object, it is because there is a belief that purpose is found in possessions. If a man sees his brother inherit a specific heirloom, he may become jealous. He is jealous not because he has any desire for the heirloom, but because he believes that his status in the family is diminished without it. Jealousy often leads to a desire to exert control over people and things out of fear. In short, it is an evaluation of self-worth fueled by fear.

Joseph, when he received his coat of many colors, was betrayed by his brothers because they were jealous. It is important to understand that they did not desire his coat: they only wanted to prove that they were of more value than he was. The coat itself exposed their jealous hearts and led them to seek an opportunity to defend their own perceived value. In this story, we see both envy and jealousy. The jealousy is highlighted in this verse: "His brothers said to him, 'Are you indeed to reign over us? Or are you indeed to rule over us?' So, they hated him even more for his dreams and for his words" (Genesis 37:8).

The brothers expressed hatred of the idea that their younger brother might have authority over them one day. They believed in their hearts that they had greater value, being older than he; but this contrasted with the dreams that God had given to Joseph. The dreams revealed that even though they were Joseph's elder brothers, Joseph would rise above them and be given an authority that he, in their eyes, didn't deserve. This inflamed his brothers' jealousy and they conspired to kill him, although they decided instead to sell him into slavery (Genesis 37:12–28). The spirit of jealousy blinded Joseph's brothers from seeing Joseph as God had made him to be. It prevented them from seeing past their fear of losing their status.

Jealousy will enter people's lives and, through false comparisons, cause them to misjudge others, inevitably laying the groundwork for destroying relationships through suspicion and fear. Jealousy becomes quickly wrapped up in possessive and obsessive attitudes that will lead people to abandon their own virtue to make room for selfish judgments and entitlement. Jealousy is a response to insecurity; it results in individuals trying to prove they have value.

When we view someone as a threat to our own self-worth, we want to defend ego at the expense of real character. For example, if someone ties their value to property ownership, and a storm destroys their property, their understanding of the world and their values become useless to them. They begin to feel that they are losing control. They will then be tempted either to seek validation by attempting to reclaim what was lost or to give in to a deep feeling of worthlessness. Such an individual cannot even value their own life apart from their possessions. By contrast, imagine someone who, once they have lost everything, begins to rebuild anew. This person stakes their worth not on their possessions but in belief and purpose.

Human behaviors are usually rooted in upbringing, culture, personal experience and a set of beliefs about the world. If someone is not grounded in the knowledge of their significance through Christ, they can quickly begin to compare themselves with others and become defensive. Jealousy is underpinned by a belief that says, "I will be replaced by someone more valuable than me." It is important to place this in context: Scripture says, "For you shall worship no other god, for the LORD, whose name is Jealous, is a jealous God" (Exodus 34:14). God knows how much He values His children; He becomes jealous towards them. He urges them to avoid replacing Him with something else and falsely perceives that any other thing as having more value than He does. In the Lord's case, this is just and righteous because His perspective is true: He does not operate from a place of fear.

The spirit of jealousy wants to blind people. It wants to blind them to the purpose God intends for them and to cause them instead to view themselves in the way they believe others see them. This spirit is not just or good because it is rooted in a false idea. Jealousy, like many spirits, lies by asking questions that have hidden assumptions in them. People who cannot see these assumptions will often think that such questions are valid. For example, the question "Why did God let this happen?" presumes that God had a hand in an outcome, when it was probably the case that He was not invited into the situation in the first place. In turn, this question undermines the idea of human free will. Even when people ask God to leave, they are acting in faith (if they believe) to receive what they ask for when they pray (Mark 11:24). Often, people indirectly ask God to leave when they try to control a situation in their own strength.

Another example of a question with a hidden assumption is "Why doesn't anyone love me enough to ...?" By asking this question, someone assumes that they are unloved, without considering likely alternatives: that others might not know how to express love to them or how to meet their needs. It may also be that they are overlooking another's expression of love because they assume that it is not genuine but manufactured. This belief will rob people of their confidence and joy, leaving them unable to feel loved.

Jealousy creates false assumptions when it prompts questions such as "What makes them better than me?" or "Why are they doing this to me?" Both questions may be blatant lies. These questions are completely self-focused and will make it impossible to understand any nuance in a situation. The first assumes that someone else is better than I am or, at least, that people perceive the other person as better, and thus leads to an answer that is a false value statement. The second implies that others are acting solely based on their desire to affect me. The answers to both questions cause me to draw comparisons between myself and others.

Whenever a spirit speaks or asks a question, it must be rejected at the level of the question, not with an answer. The only right answer is rejecting the ideas presented in the questions. Jesus often responded to the Pharisees in a way that contradicted the questions they asked. One such example is in John 9:

Some of the Pharisees near him heard these things, and said to him, "Are we also blind?" Jesus said to them, "If you were blind, you would have no guilt; but now that you say, 'We see,' your guilt remains."
(John 9:40–41)

Here, what seems to be a yes or no question obscures the fact that the answer is dependent on the belief of the person asking. It would be incomplete to simply state "yes" or "no" without context. This is important because Jesus was revealing the Pharisees' guilt by using their own words, rather than accusing them alone. He was giving them the choice to repent.

The strategy: Celebration

What is the biblical response to the spirit of jealousy? Simple, we celebrate.

Out of them shall come songs of thanksgiving,
    and the voices of those who celebrate.
    I will multiply them, and they shall not be few;
    I will make them honored, and they shall not be small.
    (Jeremiah 30:19)

We break the power of the spirit of jealousy with celebration. Celebration is how to express and capture the joy that the Lord has in each of His children. Jealousy seeks to attack joy and purpose. It wants to make people fearful, covetous, and desperate. Joy is a gift from God, so it is not something anyone can work for or capture. It is a choice that anyone can walk in or show. Celebration displays joy and sets people free from jealousy. When someone is walking in joy, they cannot be made jealous. To walk in joy, celebrate: Celebrate people; celebrate God; celebrate freedom.

In the story of Joseph, such celebrating is fully demonstrated after he and his brothers are reunited.

When Joseph saw Benjamin with them, he said to the steward of his house, "Bring the men into the house, and slaughter an animal and make ready, for the men are to dine with me at noon." The man did as Joseph told him and brought the men to Joseph's house.

(Genesis 43:16–17)

When Jacob's sons returned from Canaan to Egypt with their youngest brother, Benjamin, Joseph had an animal slaughtered and his brothers invited into his house. The purpose was to celebrate the brothers all being together once again. He displaced jealousy in his life, and in theirs, by causing them to focus on God and family. The passage concludes: "And they drank and were merry with him" (Genesis 43:34). Celebration and holding on to joy are the ways that men and women's lives can be steered towards Jesus. As the children of God, we choose to walk in joy and celebration: They displace the devil's plans and give no place to the spirit of jealousy. However, a note of caution: It is wise to guard our feelings or thoughts, when at parties or celebrations, because often the spirit of jealousy is looking for people who are not walking in joy to make them jealous of those who are.

If jealousy is a problem in a community or church, one response can be to throw a huge party to celebrate God and what He has done. Invite people to dance, sing, and rejoice, giving everyone a place to walk in joy. Proclaim joy, shout, and give praise to the Lord. Celebrate one another openly and make sure no one is left unseen. Encourage people to practice being joyful and thankful, with genuine compliments and affirmations. These are the tools that will break the spirit of jealousy. As people learn to celebrate and appreciate one another with the value that God has given them, the spirit has nothing to grasp. Honestly and openly exhort and praise God's work in their lives. Encourage people to continue to produce the fruit of the Spirit and to acknowledge the price that was paid for them to be called children of God. If anyone does not know how to celebrate someone, they should ask God for guidance because He celebrates every one of His children.

An affirmation circle is a group in which each person tells all the others, in turn, that they appreciate them. Alternatively, in larger groups, two or three people share what they find inspiring about each person. These are great ways to practice celebrating people. After an event or mission trip, try breaking up into groups of five to six to celebrate one another. These practices make leadership teams more effective as well. You can do this now in your small group. Pay attention to how people compliment and affirm one another. Genuine compliments reveal that you see something valuable that is not often mentioned or noticed.

For reflection

Here are some follow-up questions and activities for individuals or groups.

1. Take some time to form an affirmation circle. If you are leading the circle, try to take note of what people perceive and say. In future, you can encourage and champion those who may feel less seen by reminding them of what was said.
2. Which areas of your life could benefit from celebrating others?
3. Are there any traits of God that you don't celebrate?
    ◦ How can you incorporate celebrating God consistently into your life?
4. Think of a time when you became emotional because you felt slighted, disrespected, or ignored. What were you placing your value in?
5. Which virtues do you hold in high regard? Share these with others in your group. Take some time to reflect on why you might value certain virtues more than others. If another person has listed a virtue that you did not, ask them to explain why they value the virtue so highly.

CHAPTER 8

THE SPIRIT OF PRIDE AND SELF-HATRED AND THE STRATEGY OF SUBMISSION TO GOD

Since we have looked at a few different spirits already, I will confess that I was not planning to write this chapter. I felt called to write it only after coming face to face with the spirit of pride and self-hatred many times in a short period. As with all other spirits, this spirit's goal is to blind someone through sin. It tries to trap people in a gridlock in which, after a few lies are accepted as true, they are led into emotional instability from which escape seems hopeless.

Before we explore relevant Bible passages, let's look at how this spirit works. This kind of pride is not hubris, which is the type that causes someone to believe that they are better than others. This sort of pride claims to have a better perspective than God. When people decide that they can judge or evaluate themselves according to their own definition of good and evil, they partner with this spirit. They will then discard the judgment God made towards humanity at the cross of mercy; they descend into blindness where they can only understand themselves through the condemnation from this spirit. As they believe this judgment to be their own, they cling to it. The only course they feel they have is to reject God outright and embrace suicidal ideation. Suicidal ideation is when people think about killing themselves; it can range from brief thoughts to detailed plans. From this point, they have decided that their lives are of no consequence and that they are better off not existing.

This attitude might seem like an extreme form of humility; but it is pride. It is pride to stand before God and tell Him that He is wrong. It is pride to elevate our own personal perceptions and experiences above the righteous judgment of God. This mindset often leads down one of two paths: suicidal tendencies (sometimes leading to suicide) or nihilistic anger at the world. Nihilism is simply a belief that denies objective and moral truths. Without morals or truths, nihilism leads people into aggressive behaviors against themselves and society. In fact, nihilism is deeply connected to violence and self-harm; it reflects a lack of value for self, life, and others. This is because nihilism eventually results in anger: anger that is fueled by a feeling of being rejected and ignored. It is the very desire to be significant that betrays the nihilist.

The problem with this spirit is that it makes the people who agree with it unwilling to see or hear anything anyone else says. They become 'immune' to criticism. They cannot be reasoned with; and they will dismiss any attempt to love them as feeble-minded. These people become gods unto themselves.

This spirit currently has a grip on many of the world's youth and contributes to dangerous trends found among them, including not valuing life. The image they create of themselves or their place in society becomes etched in stone; and their ability to see anything outside that picture is removed. It makes its victims believe that they are irreproachable, so any form of rebuke is met with laughter and disdain. For this reason, it is wise never to engage the spirit of pride and self-hatred in conversation.

This dire problem is truly widespread. The spirit of pride and self-hatred is one of the most prolific coming against the body of Christ today. Christians must look to the word of God and root themselves in Scripture against these attacks. The Old Testament book of Jonah gives a prime example of how this spirit can manifest:

But it displeased Jonah exceedingly, and he was angry. And he prayed to the LORD and said, "O LORD, is not this what I said when I was yet in my country? That is why I made haste to flee to Tarshish; for I knew that you are a gracious God and merciful, slow to anger and abounding in steadfast love, and relenting from disaster. Therefore now, O Lord, please take my life from me, for it is better for me to die than to live."

(Jonah 4:1–3)

The prophet Jonah knew that God would show mercy to people that He had initially said should die. The spirit of pride chafed at Jonah's heart and made him angry with the Lord. In the face of God's mercy and compassion for people whom Jonah had condemned, Jonah's anger caused him to embrace suicidal ideation. He believed it would be better for him to die than for God to show mercy to His enemies. It is important to note that Jonah's suicidal ideation was not acted on. It was only in his judgment that death was better than life. This was pride. Pride was so strong in him that he did not even answer the question the Lord posed to him. This was blindness.

God asked the prophet whether it was right for him to be angry (Jonah 4:4). We do not see a response to this question. This is because pride will not allow its victims to see any viewpoint beyond their own. In this instance, Jonah could not see right or wrong: He could only feel anger that his judgment was overruled by the Lord. Although his belief was unjust, he refused to repent for the lie he believed about who deserved mercy. Later in the day, Jonah found a place to sit and the Lord, having compassion and mercy on him, caused a plant to grow to shelter him. However, in the morning, when the plant died, Jonah became angry again.

When the sun rose, God appointed a scorching east wind, and the sun beat down on the head of Jonah so that he was faint. And he asked that he might die and said, "It is better for me to die than to live." But God said to Jonah, "Do you do well to be angry for the plant?" And he said, "Yes, I do well to be angry, angry enough to die."

(Jonah 4:8–9)

Once again, Jonah is proclaiming a judgment about what is right or wrong before God. He has already placed his own view of the world above that of God. In this case, however, we see a progression: His desire for death is now being triggered by the smallest of things.

People who accept this spirit are unable to see rationally or to be reasoned with. The world becomes unjust in every way to them.

In God's justice, mercy, and compassion, Jonah saw injustice. God rebuked him accordingly, highlighting that although he did none of the work to make the plant grow, he pitied it and its death. God then compared Jonah's pity for the plant with His own view of Nineveh as a city worthy of pity. It is here that the book of Jonah ends.

We might notice that the way the passage concludes appears to be just as important as the content of the book itself. A sound argument is given and yet there is no response from Jonah. God gives perspective, and perspective is key to avoiding this trap. Although perspective is important, however, it is not the solution for fighting against this spirit, which is one that cannot be reasoned with.

The strategy: Submission to God

In Romans, it is written:

Do not be conformed to this world, but be transformed by the renewal of your mind, that by testing you may discern what is the will of God, what is good and acceptable and perfect.

(Romans 12:2)

The solution is found in renewing the mind, to prove the will of God; not to prove the will of humanity but of God alone. To examine closely this concept of renewing the mind, we must be wary of the trap of assuming that we can fully grasp this process rationally. To do so would lead back to pride. In Matthew, it says:

Then Jesus told his disciples, "If anyone would come after me, let him deny himself and take up his cross and follow me. For whoever would save his life will lose it, but whoever loses his life for my sake will find it."

(Matthew 16:24–25)

From this passage, we can see this progression:

- How do we prove the acceptable, perfect will of God? We renew our minds.
- What must we do to renew our minds? We must first desire Christ and deny ourselves.
- What does it mean to deny ourselves? In Galatians, Paul writes, "But I say, walk by the Spirit, and you will not gratify the desires of the flesh" (Galatians 5:16). So, to deny ourselves, we must walk by the Spirit. By doing so, we avoid gratifying the flesh.

Here, the solution comes not from the rational mind, but from one's spiritual walk.

From these passages, it becomes clear that knowledge and attempting to discern good and evil cannot save humanity: For to know all things would be to replace God. God's desire for relationship is shown as an invitation to come to the cross and repent. Repentance is not the promise of knowledge or clarity. Repentance is the turning away from dead works and beliefs and becoming a new creation through faith in Jesus. The renewing of the mind and wisdom become a by-product of repentance, not the means to enact it. Anyone who can be reasoned into belief can be reasoned out: Only faith is sufficient to transform someone. It is for this reason that I have a high regard for the Christian discipline of apologetics for Christian growth rather than as a form of evangelism. Like Paul, I believe that the true demonstration of the gospel is an admission of weakness and a demonstration of faith in Christ and Him crucified (1 Corinthians 2:2–5). The gospel presentation is an invitation to become part of a family: to become a brother or sister. After all, few people are convinced by arguments alone. Most respond to those that love them. If the goal is to invite someone to join our family in Christ, the most effective way is to treat them as family.

If God's will is the guiding perspective, then people cannot spend time judging other things according to their own will or experience. We seek to reconcile our beliefs and opinions with His word. By doing so, we allow the mind to undergo a process that redirects its focus from our worldly thoughts and cares. Instead, Christians take their flesh to the cross, where they find purpose, and are called to sacrifice their own desires and thoughts. The cross—and the redemption it represents—becomes the very altar where egos die. None of us can save ourselves from sin or lies without an authoritative truth; and none of us can control our own actions without changing our beliefs. A shift is needed to engage in a lifestyle that allows desire for Christ to put to death the desires of the flesh. The only way to do this is to walk by the Spirit. There is no simple, formulaic answer to conquering pride. For any attempt that we make to subdue such a spirit would only lend power to the very thing we seek to subdue. The truth is that humanity is unable to beat pride; and neither do we need to. Christ, on the other hand, does know how to destroy pride and lead people to humility.

For who knows a person's thoughts except the spirit of that person, which is in him? So also no one comprehends the thoughts of God except the Spirit of God.
   (1 Corinthians 2:11)

To deal with the spirit of pride and self-hatred, we have to expose the great ignorance that people have regarding it, and to provide the key to winning every spiritual battle we might face. Submission to Christ seems to be the only thing that breaks pride and self-hatred. However, there is no way to tell how or in what way this must be manifested.

I have, up to this point, exhorted the reader to forgive, to practice humility, to fear the Lord, and to celebrate; but, by doing so, I have not claimed any authority apart from what Scripture has shown. Christ can be the only one to break the spirit of pride and self-hatred, and submission to His will is the only solution. Any knowledge beyond this will serve to empower this spirit. But be encouraged: Reject lies about yourself and submit to Christ's lordship. Only the Spirit of God knows God's thoughts; therefore, only the Spirit of God knows His will. And if we are to walk by the Spirit of God, we need to be in communication with Him, and then our minds can begin to be renewed. By being in submission to Christ, and through the power of the Holy Spirit, Christians are set free from this treacherous and wicked spirit.

I believe in spirits; I also believe in the baptism of the Holy Spirit. I believe that if I can fill myself with the lies of false spirits, then I can be filled with the knowledge of the truth of the living God. I also believe that the only spiritual gift with which people can edify themselves is speaking in tongues. I believe, too, that sometimes, with all the gifts that we may receive from the Spirit, there can be things that prevent us from engaging with these gifts. I believe that it is beneficial to seek out the Spirit and the gift of tongues: The apostle Paul indicates tongues' fruitfulness for the human spirit (1 Corinthians 14:4). Praying in tongues contrasts with speaking foreign tongues: The former edifies the person who is praying; the other is often a tool for evangelism. In my experience, this form of edification brings a clarity of mind; praying in tongues has enriched my prayer and study of Scripture. I would encourage everyone to ask for the gift of tongues.

I do not think that speaking in tongues is the only way to walk by the Holy Spirit, but it has made my journey much easier. Neither do I believe that speaking in tongues is necessary for salvation; but it is important. Sometimes we need help to pray as we should: "For we do not know what to pray for as we ought, but the Spirit himself intercedes for us with groanings too deep for words" (Romans 8:26). I know that people in many Christian traditions will disagree with this view. I encourage the use of this gift not because I think it is necessary, but because it has saved my life. When I struggled to accept truth in Scripture, praying in tongues helped me to change my mind effortlessly and to embrace God's word. There are many gifts of the Spirit; practicing them when appropriate is of great value. For this reason, I believe that the best way we can "edify" ourselves is by praying in tongues in private. It has to be in private: It can only be in public, in a congregation, when someone with the gift of interpretation is present (see 1 Corinthians 14:27–28). Walking in the Spirit keeps us in continuous connection with God; and Paul exhorts brothers and sisters in the faith to "pray without ceasing" (1 Thessalonians 5:17).

It is not possible to grasp the knowledge of how to resist the spirit of pride; instead, submit to God while remaining open and aware of His leadership. While, as an encouragement, I have shared my Christian experience, the only solution that matters is the one that glorifies God, furthers the gospel, and sets captives free. If God leads someone else to submission in another way, I do not begrudge that: Christ exhorts me to love my family. With that command, I will submit to His lordship.

We, the body of Christ, need to weaken the hold of the spirit pride and self-hatred over our friends and families. We need to war against it by praying (in tongues or otherwise) with purpose and submitting to the lordship of Christ; and by seeking to prophesy with wisdom, which is speaking the active word of God in context and with His heart for His children. Christians ought to abandon living as if God were someone down the street or a man in the sky. He is living inside every believer. We need to become men and women who pray. And when we do not know what to pray, we should ask; and we, who have the gift, should pray in tongues. I have been most successful in leaving behind patterns of sin only after I have spent time praying in tongues. I cannot, in my own strength, change a single belief I have about the truth without the guidance of the Holy Spirit. It is for this reason that I value the gift of tongues: That is how I have experienced God. The spirit of pride and self-hatred is one that grows weak when we pray in tongues and for one another from a place of submission to God. When we walk by the Spirit, we begin to see things differently.

The spirit of pride and self-hatred feeds off people looking for answers and judging what is right and wrong apart from God's word. The moment someone forms a personal plan of action against it; they inevitably partner with it. Any attempt to determine the solution though human means will fail. Only dependence on God and surrender can drive this spirit out. Knowledge of good and evil was the consequence of the first sin, which was the temptation to be like God. To make this clearer, we could say that when we judge something as good or evil apart from God, we take the place of God; the only righteous judgment we can have is that of discerning what is consistent with what God has declared as good or evil. By doing so, we depend on the objective moral law of God. To believe we know good or evil—apart from the knowledge revealed by God—is the product of the fall of humanity.

Therefore, God measures the heart. The state of the heart determines whether anyone is in sin because of the lies they believe or because they submit to an authority that is not God. So, when someone decides in their heart what is good apart from God, they must, in turn, reject God and His word, and so inevitably leave His presence.

In conclusion, the only way to return to God is to embrace His word as true and, as the bride of Christ, to say, "We neither know nor understand Your thoughts and ways; but we will trust in You with all that we are" (see Isaiah 55:8–9). By doing so, the church can break ungodly patterns of behavior and belief. This is a product of obedience and submission to His Spirit: that all might know His will and prove it as good; a perfect will on display in each person's life. It is in this place that relationship with Christ begins anew; and everyone can once again go before God. There, we believers can ask Him questions, express pain, and seek answers. No one can understand or know why God forgives those whom He forgives or His motivation for doing what He does: at least, not until they ask Him with the intention of seeking His heart on a matter. If we believe that we are right and He is wrong, we will never have communion with Him because we will be unable to ask Him anything or hear His answers.

For reflection

Here are some follow-up questions and activities for individuals or groups.

1. What are some ways that you submit to God and demonstrate His lordship in your life?
2. Are there any beliefs you struggle with that seem to be evident in Scripture?
   - Have you prayed or fasted to receive answers?
   - Do you need to know the answer to serve God and trust Him?
3. How can we acknowledge the value or significance God has placed on others?
4. Do you know God's purpose for your life?
   - Is it rooted in scripture?
   - If you don't know God's purpose, take some time to find some Bible passages that point to the purpose and value of humanity. Romans, Ephesians, and Hebrews touch on this topic.
5. How can you partner with God's purpose for you?
6. Part of submission is repentance. In what ways can you repent on behalf of your city or community? (I would not repent for an individual unless led by God because it would require judging the person.)
7. Learning and repentance are both forms of submission. To practice submitting to God's word, pick a topic in Scripture (for example, altars, sacrifice, holy days or the exodus). Take some time to read and pray about it. Ask God for new revelation about the topic.

CHAPTER 9

THE UNDERLYING SPIRITUAL CAUSES: FEAR AND PRIDE

Since we have examined the five strategies of forgiveness, humility, fear of the Lord, celebration, and submission to God for combating specific types of evil, this chapter does not revisit them. Here, I want to reveal the workings of the spiritual realm so that we may be confident when engaging in any type of spiritual warfare.

Behind each of the five spirits, we see common themes. The most prominent is that each spirit is a direct manifestation of some form of fear, and it causes sin by inflaming human pride. One way of thinking about sin is to imagine a building that is established on a foundation of fear and that has a frame of human pride. The fear sets the stage for a sinful response, but pride shapes the response. Demonic forces are not the primary enemy of Christianity or Christians. The primary enemies are sin and death. The demons were not the ones who tempted Cain; but, rather, sin and death were present in Cain because of what Adam and Eve did in the Garden of Eden (Genesis 4:7). As a consequence of death, we are trained from birth to view the world through a lens of fear. The first thing parents try to instill in children is what to do or not do to avoid death. This fear forces us to think continuously about ourselves and our safety, leading to the development of pride. Pride is how we learn to protect ourselves from danger. In Christ, we relinquish that fear of death, follow Him (even if it may cost us our lives), and trust in the promise of eternal life.

Let's review each spirit, one at a time.

The spirit of hatred

The spirit of hatred might arise from a fear of the unknown, a fear of being overlooked, or a fear due to feeling marginalized. It's not hard to imagine that fear leads to hatred. Human pride partners with fear to create false beliefs or viewpoints that dehumanize those it hates. These beliefs place humanity above the laws and statutes of God. More significantly, it is only God who has the right to prescribe death; so, when this spirit provokes murder, the individual either becomes their own god or has submitted to a god other than Jesus.

The spirit of lust

The spirit of lust can come from a fear of not having enough, a fear of missing out, a fear of being unhappy, or a fear of being alone. It encourages men and women to devalue others as they pursue their own goals.

The spirit of witchcraft

The spirit of witchcraft can come from a fear of loss of control, a fear of subjugation, or a fear of not receiving what one desires. Witchcraft is a practice that declares rebellion against God and is based on a belief of what someone thinks they deserve, which can only come from pride.

The spirit of jealousy

The spirit of jealousy can be linked to a fear of others' evaluation of our status, a fear of being abused, or any other fear that tries to preserve a sense of entitlement. This spirit engages human pride by encouraging the man or woman to believe lies about their own identity and, as with witchcraft, what they think they deserve.

The spirit of pride and self-hatred

The spirit of pride and self-hatred often stems from the fear of being worthless. This spirit uses pride to reshape the way in which people judge themselves.

The common trait: The spirit of fear

So, the spirit of fear can help to establish each of these other spirits. This is because fear is a belief (if I fear death, I believe that I am susceptible to death). We have already touched on how belief is tied to behavior and what individuals manifest. Beliefs can possess entire communities; these beliefs are manifestations of spirits. The good news is that we don't need a new strategy to undo the work of these spirits. If fear is a belief, then faith can replace fear.

Faith conquers fear

Faith in what, though? Scripture says, "For God gave us a spirit not of fear but of power and love and self-control" (2 Timothy 1:7). This verse provides the answer: It's not the gift being given; it's the giver. We believe in God for who He is; the One who is giving the Spirit has the most significance in this verse. When Christians receive what God promises them, they won't pick up fear. Someone who focuses on believing in a God who provides, a God of the impossible, a God who fights for them, and a God who died for their transgressions simply won't have time for fear. Every opportunity to fear is an opportunity to look at God and know His character.

The Bible says that we are each a new creation in Christ (2 Corinthians 5:17; Ephesians 4:23–24; Colossians 3:10). If I hold on to the belief that I am a victim, I will play that role. If I believe that I am a sinner, I will reject my identity as a new creation and do what sinners do: sin. If sin is separation from God, the most effective self-evaluation is to discern where I am not in union with God. The goal of being sinless makes sense only from a relational standpoint rather than that of personal status. It will always be pride that declares itself to be sinless; but as sons and daughters of God, we will let God declare what we are on Judgment Day. If we, as Christians, believe that we are subject to sin and death, we will submit. Paul exhorts believers to die to sin (Romans 6:11) so that we may be alive to God. Faith is how we journey with God, as 2 Corinthians 5:7 says, "for we walk by faith, not by sight."

Transformation is a matter of belief and not a matter of knowledge. While there is some threshold of knowledge required to believe something, it is only the belief that is lived out. We do not exist to know all things: We exist to represent God as image-bearers. We can only look like Him if we hold Him in our gaze.

When you next feel fear whispering about a worst-case scenario, try not to build your words and actions on something that isn't real or that is, at best, an incomplete representation of the situation. Instead, find a Bible passage and stand on what is real. If fear says, "You will never amount to anything," respond with

For I know the plans I have for you, declares the LORD, plans for welfare and not for evil, to give you a future and a hope. Then you will call upon me and come and pray to me, and I will hear you. You will seek me and find me, when you seek me with all your heart.

(Jeremiah 29:11–13)

If fear says, "No one will ever love you," respond with

For God so loved the world, that he gave his only Son, that whoever believes in him should not perish but have eternal life. For God did not send his Son into the world to condemn the world, but in order that the world might be saved through him.

(John 3:16–17)

There are countless examples of this use of Scripture. When Scripture becomes the meditation of your heart (Joshua 1:8), you will prosper. Belief is the foundation; it is the beginning of the battle. Belief is the fundamental requirement to be successful in any form of warfare: Soldiers who don't think they can win a battle will likely lose it.

In concluding this discourse on spirits, I want to end by encouraging us to make Christ the focus of our belief. If we pray for healing, we are really seeking an encounter with the Healer. If we pray for deliverance, we are really seeking the intervention of the Lord of Hosts. If we pray for comfort, we are really seeking to be embraced by the only

One who knows our hearts. Let the focus of our belief be on a Person, not a circumstance. If all we need is a miracle, then there is no glory for God in our breakthrough. If we need only an answer, there is no relationship to be had. It's important not to limit how God wants to reveal Himself. We invite Him to have His way and let Him take the lead.

For reflection

Here are some follow-up questions and activities for individuals or groups.

1. Which areas of sin have you struggled with in the past?
   - Identify the fear and the pride that led to sin.
2. As a group, pick a sin. Take turns to come up with possible fears that might lead to that sin or belief.
   - How many different types of fear are there?
   - Is there a statement or root that can summarize each of those specific fears?
3. If pride is holding ungodly beliefs, which aspects of culture do you think of as types of pride?
4. Pick out a verse to memorize and stand on. Remember, if we are made in the image of Christ, and Christ is the Word, then the Word of God is a description of who God made us to be.
5. Think of the fruit of the spirit. What kinds of beliefs are consistent with each part of the fruit? Try to identify one belief about God for each part of the fruit.

CHAPTER 10

DEFINING A VIRTUE

We have established the importance of responding to spirits by practicing what is taught in Scripture. Living a godly life, believing in God's word, and practicing virtue through faith in Christ are at the core of spiritual warfare. Christians advance the kingdom through evangelism, ministry, healing, and casting out demons. The kingdom of God (Revelation 1:6) is made up of "believers;" we are so called because we believe.

We have looked at vices and spirits that oppose Christ. However, from only a cursory glance at this topic, it is clear that to wage war against these spirits, Christians ought not to leave any room for them. We leave no room by recognizing what God has called evil and what God has said is good. To do so, we first dispense with the notion that any person on their own can define what is good. Many modern Christians would likely err on the side of humanist Christianity. The problem with this way of thinking is that it falls short of the teachings of Christ, as an examination of Scripture would show. The chief end of Christianity concerns the glory of God. The benefit to humanity is a by-product, not the primary product: "But seek first the kingdom of God and his righteousness, and all these things will be added to you" (Matthew 6:33). Updating the teachings and practices of Christ by injecting our own ideas into Scripture is dangerous. The Bible warns:

. . .

Now the Spirit expressly says that in later times some will depart from the faith by devoting themselves to deceitful spirits and teachings of demons, through the insincerity of liars whose consciences are seared.

(1 Timothy 4:1–2)

By creating new doctrines, people willingly participate with spirits, just as Eve did when she listened to the serpent who tempted her with the promise that she could "be like God" (Genesis 3:5). In this context, believers do not need to redefine good but, rather, submit to the good that has already been established through Christ's ministry, which was made plain in the Scriptures. And rather than deconstructing belief using the world's questions to do so, we can ask if the Bible does what it promises when it is applied appropriately. Also, we, as Christians, must be critical of any "new" doctrine; we should examine it and follow it to its logical conclusion to see if it does, in fact, produce fruit compatible with the Bible's teaching.

To do so, we should first attempt to define a virtue. For instance, we may say that love is good, according to Scripture. If that is true, is love a noun, a verb, or some other construct existing outside language? Scripture states that "God is love" (1 John 4:8). Is Scripture therefore telling its readers, redundantly, that God is good? What defines a virtue? If love is a noun, can it also be a verb, an action? These questions may give anyone pause in their exploration of virtue or—as the Bible calls it— "fruit."

CAVE

My goal is to take the Bible's teachings and make them straightforward and memorable. Here, I introduce an acronym that can help us to navigate defining a virtue, make it easier to grasp, and establish a simple way to practice it and grow. The acronym is CAVE.

First, define the **characteristic**: We establish which virtue we want or wish to improve. Second, take **action**: Any virtue we seek to acquire or improve should change our actions and be visible to others through our altered behavior. Third is the **value statement**: From examining the virtue itself alongside the actions that represent it, we can define how best to express and capture what we mean when we refer to the characteristic. Lastly, **exercise**: We plan which daily actions to incorporate into our lives, to establish this virtue effectively in our system of belief. A helpful example of how to apply CAVE is given in the following table.

TABLE 1: CAVE:

Characteristic	Honesty
Actions	• Avoid lying. • Avoid deception, e.g. not distracting others from my true intentions by giving more or less information than is necessary. • Avoid misrepresenting my intentions through a deceptive use of language.
Value Statement	I want to represent myself as truthfully and accurately as I can so that people may see my true intentions.
Exercise	• Answer questions concisely and accurately. • Speak openly about my real desires. • Express myself in a clear, straightforward manner when asked questions. • Not to take significant action without being able to explain to others my true reasons.

As we begin to build these virtues into our lives, we will inevitably discover that being good people according to Scripture will never be possible outside Christ: For the actions we manage to suppress will reveal new problems through other behaviors. There is no single formula for becoming good.

ROPE

However, to take the steps found in Scripture, believers need more than a helpful way to grasp virtue. We require another useful acronym: ROPE. It aids in addressing our emotional side as we seek to grow in character. After all, we are a mix of the logical and the emotional, and little is achieved without changing the whole person.

First, R stands for **repent**: We confess our sins before God and another person, reaffirming our commitment to God through seeking the forgiveness of sins. This free forgiveness is offered because our God sent Jesus to die for the sins of all humanity. We can never be grateful enough for this act: It allows us to walk in freedom and to choose righteousness.

Next is O for **observe**: We examine all thoughts, beliefs, and unforgiveness that lead to the behaviors or actions that prevent us from walking in the values or virtues we seek. Knowing the source empowers us to repent effectively or address the ideas preventing progress.

Then, P is for **pray**: We ask God to give us wisdom about the problems that hold us back. Why is the belief that is held a lie? What is true? Is there something that God is asking of us? Is there something that God is offering us to replace that belief? To avoid reproducing a false idea of what goodness is in our own hearts, we ask these questions honestly and scripturally. The goal is to represent Christ.

Finally, E is for **end agreement**: We openly express that we will no longer partner with lies or unforgiveness. We will instead choose to agree with Christ, scripture states that people are able to receive forgiveness only when they willingly forgive others (Matthew 18:21-35); and faith is in service to God only when people believe the truth (John 4:23).

TABLE 2: ROPE

Repentance	Lord, I repent of my dishonest behaviors. I ask for Your forgiveness and Your grace as starting today to live an honest life, glorifying You.
Observation	Reasons I am dishonest: • I fear what others think. • I fear failing. • I desire revenge on those who wrong me.
Prayer	Lord, in light of these things, I pray for wisdom to see where the root of my unbelief is. Show me which lies I have partnered with. Show me how they prevent me from being honest. Reveal to me Your wisdom in this matter.
End to Agreement	Lord, I reject the lie that I need to live or believe a certain way to make people happy. The only one I need to serve is You. I break my agreement with the lie that I need to protect myself. Thank You, God, for setting me free from dishonesty and equipping me to be honest before You.

ROPE can help us to organize how we think about virtue and the areas of our lives where healing is needed. It is not a new doctrine: It is a repackaging of what is already revealed in Scripture; but it is something that can help those who attempt to use it seriously.

Instead of deconstructing our faith by questioning the claims, found in Scripture, that set us free from sin and make each of us a new creation, we question if belief in Christ produces the fruit it claims to produce. I believe this form of examining our faith, and what we believe, produces a more reliable witness to the faith than deconstructing without engaging with its core doctrines. If the truth found in Scripture can redeem our souls, then we have all the evidence we need of its validity. The claims Scripture makes are true and trustworthy; they are evident in the outcome of practicing them.

For reflection

To review this chapter, use CAVE and ROPE. Share your notes with other group members so that they can hold you accountable for exercising virtue through belief.

SOME FINAL THOUGHTS

I do hope this book has helped you and your community. We have seen that every spirit not of God wants to blind us. The five I have highlighted have much in common because of how they work and how they partner with a sixth, the spirit of fear. Each one causes us to focus on something related to who we are: Hatred focuses on our being offended, lust on our desire, witchcraft on our agency, jealousy on our self-worth, and pride and self-hatred on our self-evaluation. For hatred, we forgive and remove the offense that has held us in place. With lust, we embrace humility and focus on the needs of others; doing so prevents us from being wrapped up in our own desires. With witchcraft, we practice the fear of the Lord and speaking the truth of God. In the case of jealousy, we celebrate and hold fast to joy, never letting our value as human beings come into question. For self-hatred and pride, we abandon our false beliefs about ourselves in pursuit of being obedient to Christ.

Effective spiritual warfare and growth happen when we learn to ask the right questions and reject the assumptions that bad questions bring. A good question is one that does not assume the motives of another but rather seeks to understand a person or circumstance. A bad question is one that assumes the answer or motive before the question is addressed. It is important to ask God, when dealing with any spirit, how we should move, think, or believe. Often, we do not need to fight a spiritual battle head on: It is of greater benefit to cut the enemy off at the root before his influence can grow.

Love God, love people, and love truth.

AUTHOR'S NOTE AND INVITATION

If you have just finished reading this first edition, I would like to invite you to collaborate with me to create a collection of testimonies. I decided not to include any personal stories in this version because I wanted my readers to engage with *Spirit War* in a unique way. I would like you to try out the strategies to see whether you have success or encounter God. For the second edition, I plan to write a subsequent part to each chapter filled with testimonies of people who put the strategies into practice. I want your stories to encourage the body about the power of God.

If you would like to contribute your testimony to the second edition, please email it to simplestrategies.jal@gmail.com. If I feel led to include your story in *Spirit War*, I will follow up by sending you a form authorizing me to use your testimony and add your name to the list of collaborators, which you can sign and return. To keep the individuals mentioned in your pieces anonymous, we can work together to change dates, places, ages, and so on. Once I have received enough submissions, I will publish the second edition, and the book will be complete.

In the future, I hope to produce more books on spiritual warfare and other topics, as the Lord leads. Thank you so much for taking the time to read this book. I hope it has blessed you.

Shalom.